50
bandag
ESTABLISHED 1957

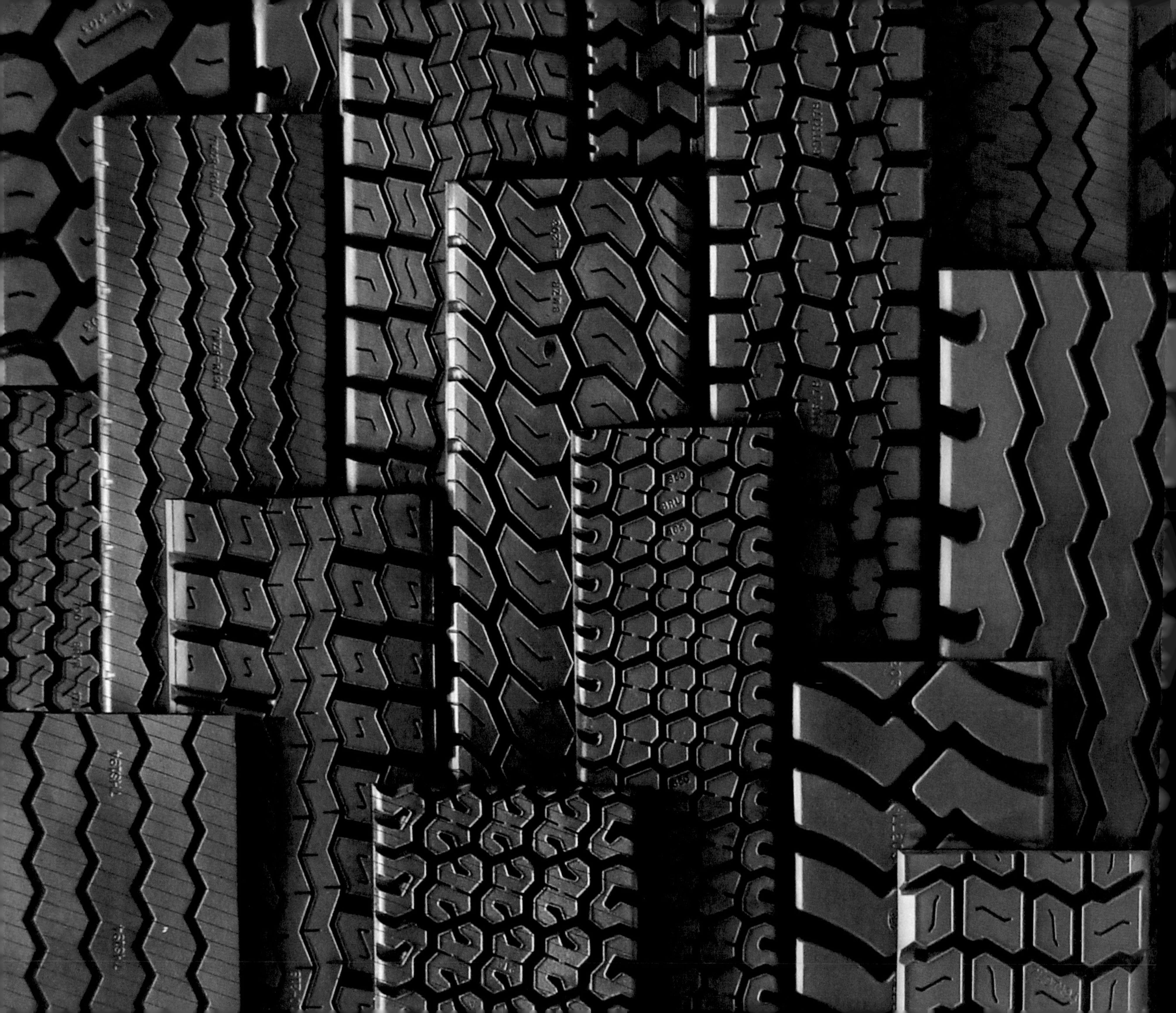

# REVOLUTIONS

## *Bandag's 50 Years of Innovation in the Tire Industry*

C. Randall Heuston

WDG Publishing

# REVOLUTIONS

*Bandag's 50 Years of Innovation in the Tire Industry*

| | |
|---|---|
| Creative Direction | Duane Wood |
| Design/Art Direction | Eric Johnson |
| Photo/Editorial Research | Bandag Communications Group |



First published in the United States of America by
WDG Communications Inc.
401 First Street SE
Suite 102
Post Office Box 1115
Cedar Rapids, Iowa 52406-1115
Telephone (319) 396-1401
Facsimile (319) 396-1647

Library of Congress Cataloging-in-Publication Data

Heuston, C. Randall.
Bandag revolutions : Bandag's 50 years of innovation in the tire industry/C. Randall Heuston.
p. cm.
ISBN 978-0-9793779-2-1 (alk. paper)
1. Automobiles–Tires–History. 2. Tire industry–History. I. Title.
TL270.H48 2007
338.7'678320973–dc22
2007035565

Printed in the United States of America

10 9 8 7 6 5 4 3 2 1

# TABLE *of* CONTENTS

F O R E W O R D

# A REVOLUTIONARY COMPANY

With a blast of its horn, a shiny 18-wheeler runs through the gears out of Tacoma on its long haul to Atlanta. As that huge truck, loaded to what weigh stations will allow, rolls along our nation's interstates, its 18 wheels will turn thousands and thousands of revolutions on this trip alone.

The integrity of those wheels and tires hardly gets a second thought from anybody outside the trucking industry. But, if you do think about it, the reliability of those wheels and tires correlates with economic prosperity. The more successful revolutions, the more products are delivered on time, the more money and services are exchanged, and the greater the contributions to quality of life.

Throughout most of its 50-year history, Bandag, headquartered in Muscatine, Iowa, has been the world's leading retread tire products manufacturer and supplier. Bandag, in recent decades, has controlled up to 45 percent of the retread market. The company's success owes to the fact that its quality products and services have lowered the cost of those truck wheel revolutions, further contributing to the nation's economic growth and stability.

You do the math. A trucking company wants to outfit one of its rigs with new tires at about $350 a pop. To put new tires on an 18-wheeler, they're looking at more than $6,000. But if they retread those tires for about $100 apiece, they've sliced the investment by 70 percent. What's more, they can safely retread a tire two or three times. Trucking companies in North America alone save an estimated $2 billion annually using retreaded tires. That's huge because tire costs represent the third largest expense of those truck fleets' operating budgets.

Also, retreaded tires reduce our nation's dependence on oil. According to the Tire Retread Information Bureau, it takes 22 gallons of oil to make a new truck tire, while retreading a tire requires only seven gallons; that's because most of the oil to make a new tire goes into the casing, which is reused in a retread.

Without truck tire retreads the nation's dependence on oil would rise, and the cost of many consumer and commercial products and activities would, too — everything from groceries to retail merchandise to new home construction to heavy equipment manufacturing. Retreaded tires play a significant, though mostly unnoticed, role in sustaining the world economy.

But other kinds of revolution are demanded of those doing business in and with the transportation industry, and the success of those revolutions likewise determines the prosperity of fleet owners, truck drivers, mechanics, rubber manufacturers, tire distributors and many, many others along the supply chain. These kinds of revolutions are not only in the technology of production processes but also in ways of doing business so as to meet ever-changing customer needs and often unpredictable market demands.

The story of Bandag is about more than innovation in retread tire production and distribution, although that in itself is worth telling. It's really a story about innovation and continual improvement in ways of serving customers, cultivating business relationships to gain competitive advantage, and preserving high core business values while reacting with agility to new demands of increasingly turbulent markets.

The first chapter of the Bandag story lasted a decade. Riding the vision and sheer grit of its founder, Bandag endured many early failures and overcame intimidating challenges on the strength of its self-driven technological innovation. By the mid-'60s, it was a profitable company with a growing reputation for quality products and solid customer support.

The next 25 years or so, beginning with Bandag's initial public stock offering, were characterized by further innovation, dramatic global expansion, new products, wide-ranging services, effective dealer training and strategic alignment, and market dominance. Bandag rolled into the ranks of the Fortune 500, and the road ahead looked straight and smooth. The sound you heard was investors applauding.

However, the marketplace seldom lets a company just keep doing what it's always done, no matter how well it's done it. By the mid-'90s it became apparent Bandag would have to reinvent itself to deal with a global economy characterized by fierce competition as well as profound changes in the trucking industry such as deregulation, consolidation and the growth of leasing. Again, Bandag rose to the challenge, strengthening its Strategic Alliance with dealers and gradually becoming more vehicle centric than tire centric. The emphasis was on selling solutions, providing an ever-growing number of fleet services, rather than only products. Yet the battle was far from over.

As the 21st century arrived and its 50th anniversary approached, Bandag's products, processes, services and dealer network — indeed, its entire way of doing business — continued to face challenge and uncertainty, owing to still more aggressive competition and disruptive external economic conditions. Bandag went on record as reaffirming its core values, innovation topping the list, and pledging to perform to the level of its refocused vision. Bandag was still a very solid and profitable company, but it was no longer gobbling up market share.

In December 2006, Bandag and Bridgestone Americas Holding, Inc., long involved as business partners on several fronts, announced a merger that would make Bandag a wholly owned subsidiary of Bridgestone Americas. It was lauded by the corporate offices as "a good fit," but Bandag employees, dealers, fleet owners and others woke up to face additional unknowns. Was their success and security with Bandag soon to be gone with the wind? Surely, Bandag will be a different company in the decades ahead.

Still, the fact Bandag became an appealing acquisition for the world's largest producer of tires and rubber products — Bridgestone became that after it took over Firestone several years earlier — says a lot about Bandag's culture of excellence and bottom-line success. It says that Bandag's record of reinvention, revolting against complacency and disdaining the status quo, holds promise of good things to come for those associated with the company from here on.

It all makes for an intriguing story because Bandag's spirit and business practice has proved to be, by any definition, downright revolutionary.

— C. Randall Heuston

MERRY CHRISTMAS

CHAPTER ONE:

DOUBLE THE MILEAGE GUARANTEED

# A PRODUCT THAT SHOOK THE WORLD

*Like many other classic business success stories, Bandag's begins with the vision of a single entrepreneur.*

*Roy J. Carver — who some would say sprang from the mold of strong-willed American industrialists like Cornelius Vanderbilt, Henry Ford and John D. Rockefeller — locked in on the idea that something ready to be tossed aside could be recycled and made better than the original. Carver's vision, focused first on industrial pumps, famously shifted to rubber tires.*

*"Opportunity is missed by most people," Thomas Edison said, "because it is dressed in overalls and looks like work." True, to many eyes used tires may seem a mundane prospect, but Carver saw dollar signs. When a tire's original tread wears down, the casing may still be good for thousands of more miles. Why throw them away? That's what was happening, more often than not, before Roy Carver came along.*

The farm boy turned pump manufacturer in little Muscatine, Iowa, was always looking to do things better. He grew up wearing overalls, and he wasn't afraid of work. Carver had worked his way through high school and college, and along the way he coupled his natural curiosity with an obsession about craftsmanship and product quality. And he could see the future.

Just as Vanderbilt foresaw a nationwide railroad network, and helped lay the tracks for it, Carver understood that the trucking industry needed reliable and affordable tires to efficiently carry products to far-flung market destinations. He grew up in the Great Depression and "saw families with little children living off pickings at the city dump." His vision was not just about personal profits but about providing jobs and better living conditions in his community. So, when he discovered in Germany what he thought was a tire retreading process superior to anything used in the United States, he jumped to buy the patent rights and formed Bandag, Incorporated.

That was December 1957, 50 years ago.

Roy and Lucille Carver pose proudly in 1957 with the first Bandag retread built in the USA using the Bandag retread process.

*"The Bandag concept was so revolutionary, and there were plenty of skeptics. Mr. Carver stuck with Bandag when many others would have given up or sold out."*
*– Ron Seiler*

Only months later Carver set up his first manufacturing operation in a vacant sauerkraut factory on the edge of Muscatine, with his Carver Pump Co. and Carver Foundry Products providing the equipment. He was convinced Bandag would be highly profitable and bring significant cost-savings to the transportation industry for decades to come. That predicted success, though, came neither immediately nor easily.

Carver reinforced his vision with sheer grit. The saying among Bandag employees was, "If you tell Roy Carver something can't be done, he'll do it just to prove you wrong."

Ron Seiler, one Bandag's first managers, remembers that incredible Carver tenacity. "When we started, Bandag didn't have a proven system. The concept was so revolutionary, and there were plenty of skeptics. Mr. Carver stuck with Bandag when many others would have given up or sold out." Indeed, Carver put his profitable Carver Pump Co. at risk, leveraging it nearly to bankruptcy to prop up the fledgling tire company.

Carver was very much a hands-on manager in those early days. He attended the University of Illinois in engineering, he worked long hours, showed up at the plants unannounced, asked about details,

A successful pump manufacturer, Roy Carver used the profits from Carver Pump Co. to establish Bandag, Incorporated. "We almost brought Carver Pump to its knees in developing Bandag," Carver said. "But we got through it."

IOWA
SECRETARY OF STATE
CERTIFICATE OF INCORPORATION

This Certificate of Incorporation, dated December 20, 1957, represents Bandag's birth certificate.

Bandag's first retread plant was originally a vacant sauerkraut factory purchased from Tooman Canning in Muscatine, Iowa. In 1958 Bandag operations began here with a handful of employees. The plant was used to prepare tread rubber for shipment to Bandag dealers.

scrutinized pieces of rubber, and personally initiated many of the improvements that got the company off the ground. He is credited with developing the flexible rubber curing envelope, one of the early Bandag innovations, eliminating heavy metal bands. (Later, when radial tires came on the scene, this development allowed Bandag to retread radials without missing a beat; radial tires could not be economically recapped in the rigid molds used by many of Bandag's competitors.) As Carver later recalled, "We started up doing the very best we knew how." From the beginning, the emphasis was on quality.

And because Carver's co-workers shared his vision, they, too, became "radically dedicated" to making it reality. "We were involved in a new venture — which was an *adventure* — and when the vision was put in front of people," Seiler says, "they wanted to be part of it.

*"All the problems created a certain magic, and everybody pulled together.... We shared the belief we were changing the American tire industry."*
*– Frank Nelson*

We all took it very personally when things didn't work." The small band of believers was truly on a mission, working overtime and weekends, sometimes to exhaustion and often without extra pay, summoning their strength and ingenuity to solve daunting production and financial problems.

Ed Kopf, a 40-year Bandag employee, recalls when they "were trying to perfect the one-ply cushion gum. I had worked a 16-hour day and gone home to rest. About six o'clock that night my phone rang, and the voice on the other end was Mr. Carver's. He told me to get back down to the plant. So I went, and we worked all night on trying to perfect the manufacture of the one-ply cushion. I didn't get home until 11 o'clock the next morning."

Frank Nelson, another who played several key roles in the early history of Bandag, remembers: "All the problems created a certain magic, and everybody pulled together. We became close-knit teams, more like a family than employees. We shared the belief we were changing the American tire industry."

Just as Henry Ford didn't invent the first automobile but revolutionized automobile production, so Bandag came on line while another retread process was already in place. It was called "hot capping," but it was flawed in concept and unreliable; its rigid metal molds didn't tolerate subtle differences in tire sizes, making the process inflexible.

What's more, a lot of recapping then used rubber compounds of inferior quality. Carver said, "I wanted to use the best materials money could buy."

In contrast to the prevailing hot cap processes that cured the tread to the casing at high temperatures, the Bandag system bonds extremely tough, pre-cured rubber treads to tire casings at relatively low temperature so as not to weaken the used casings. The result, after years of trial and error, was a retreaded tire that far out-performed the competition.

Martin G. Carver, one of Roy's sons and former president, chairman and CEO, says Bandag's success in its first decade can be largely attributed not only to his father's perseverance but also to the "genius" of Edwin T. Brodie, Jr. Roy Carver had recruited Brodie, a research and development engineer, from B.F. Goodrich Co.

Ed Brodie's innovative solutions in the Bandag system were many, including significant improvement to the basic bonding procedure. The original patent Carver purchased from Bernard Nowak in Germany relied upon a bonding cement,

No. 3,236,709

THE UNITED STATES OF AMERICA

TO ALL TO WHOM THESE PRESENTS SHALL COME:

Whereas Roy James Carver, of Muscatine, Iowa, assignor to Bandag Incorporated, of Muscatine, Iowa, a corporation of Iowa,

presented to the Commissioner of Patents a petition praying for the grant of Letters Patent for an alleged new and useful invention the title and a description of which are contained in the specification of which a copy is hereunto annexed and made a part hereof, and complied with the various requirements of Law in such cases made and provided, and

Whereas upon due examination made the said Claimant is adjudged to be justly entitled to a patent under the Law.

Now therefore these Letters Patent are to grant unto the said Bandag Incorporated, its successors or assigns for the term of Seventeen years from the date of this grant the right to exclude others from making, using or selling the said invention throughout the United States.

In testimony whereof I have hereunto set my hand and caused the seal of the Patent Office to be affixed at the City of Washington this twenty-second day of February, in the year of our Lord one thousand nine hundred and sixty-six, and of the Independence of the United States of America the one hundred and ninetieth.

Attest:

One of the many U.S. Patents Bandag would receive for its innovative research and development of the retread process.

B E R N A R D   N O W A K — R O Y   C A R V E R

Bernard A. Nowak, the German pioneer of retreading, and Roy Carver pose during one of Roy's many visits to Germany.

Bernard Nowak was a hands-on owner. He built retreads in his plant in Darmstadt, Germany.

## Whence the Bandag Name?

One of the provisions of the deal in 1957 between Bernard A. Nowak and Roy J. Carver was that the name Bandag be retained to describe the retread process and products. The word "band" in German means what it does in English, in this case a band of rubber, and AG is an abbreviation for Aktien Gesellsaft, or "Co., Ltd."; thus Bandag means "band company." By most accounts, the inventor felt the name had a personal connection as well. "BAN," were his initials, and the "D" stood for Darmstadt, Nowak's home town, where he had started his company. Thus: *Bernard Anton Nowak Darmstadt Company.* ▪

which was later replaced by a marginally more effective two-ply cushion gum. Then Ed Brodie invented a single-ply cushion gum, HD30, which, with ongoing improvements, is the bonding material still used today. It was a breakthrough.

Under Ed Brodie's direction, Bandag research and development never let up, and additional patents followed. Eventually scores of tread designs were developed, meeting governmental regulations, including noise restrictions, and addressing a wide variety of application-specific needs. Of course, the market never stayed constant, but the company was small enough to be quick on its feet, reacting well to whatever came along. Bandag processes and products just kept getting better.

Carver recalled that competition was fierce in the early days. "The recappers banded against us, so I went directly to the truckers. I told them to use our tires, and if they weren't happy with them, they didn't have to pay for them." The strategy was risky, but it worked.

In the early years many tread designs were copied. Here, however, Herb Roelle and John Burche of Bandag's research and development group hold the drawings of Brawny® tread, a Bandag patented original.

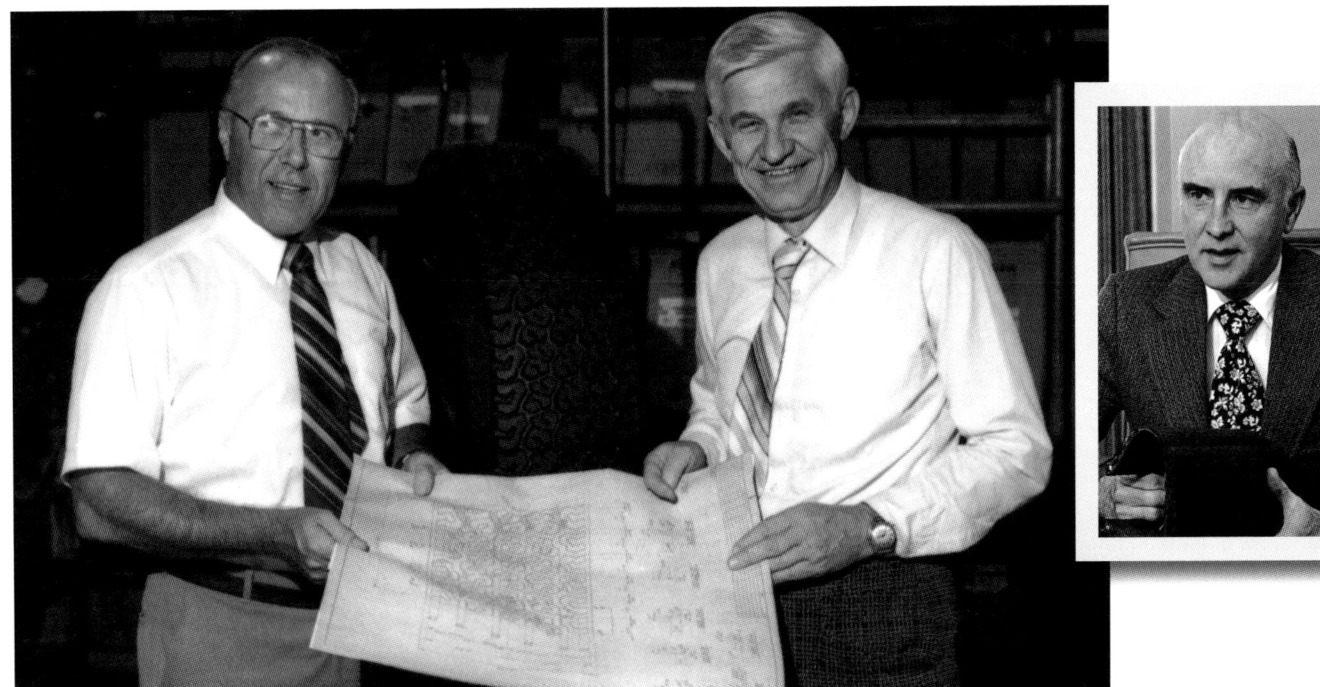

Bandag's Chief Chemist, Ed Brodie, had a profound impact on the company. He was responsible for over 100 patents and applications in over 25 foreign countries, including the pressure chamber, single-ply cushion gum and MICRO-SIPE® process tread.

This brick house, located across from Plant 2 on Muscatine's Hershey Ave., became the first Bandag Research and Development Center. The Center utilized the latest in available technology in the humblest of settings.

Herb Roelle, an engineer responsible for some of the early Bandag machine designs, recalled, "Those were colorful times, no question. We had a certain camaraderie — everybody saving one another. We had a sense of loyalty. People who came to work here stayed here. And we were always trying to outsmart the bigger companies."

As Nelson, who decades later was called up for the Gulf War because of his tire expertise, likes to say, "If the average guy would walk, we would run. If the other guy would run, we would sprint.... We were called 'the bastards of the tire industry'... and I guess we were."

To beat the competition Bandag had to create a closely monitored, closed production system for its retreads — formulating and testing its own rubber compounds, bonding materials and tread designs, producing the most durable tread rubber ever seen, and designing and manufacturing machines and tools to meet the demands of the "cold-cured" retread process. The emphasis in the Bandag system was not on cheap input costs but on the highest possible quality, and Bandag knew it couldn't always depend on outside suppliers to uphold its rigorous standards.

Carver said, "I can't make myself turn out a lousy product; that's just part of my nature. I don't want to do anything I'm not proud of." That proved to be his company's motto as well. And once Bandag products were proven, Bandag didn't run the price up. Bill Block, director of corporate communications, said: "Carver felt that being the best doesn't entitle you to run the price sky high; just make a fair profit."

However, it wasn't the horizontally integrated, high quality production process but rather the vertical integration of research, production, marketing, sales, dealer support, and distribution that was the dynamic force in Bandag's success. After Standard Oil mastered oil refining, Rockefeller and his company vertically integrated everything from extraction to refining to transporting to marketing and distributing.

W.G. McDowell of Kansas City was among the first to become a Bandag dealer. He admired the ambition and determination of Roy Carver. McDowell said Carver would fly in and hang around the shop looking for ideas and solving problems.

Carver followed a similar principle, selling and supporting franchises of his retread system to independent tire dealers. (Later fleet owners desiring in-house retread plants would join this multi-faceted partnership.) He established the first such franchise barely six months after acquiring the North American patent rights.

The dealers would not only sell Bandag® retreads but actually do the retreading in their own shops, exclusively using machines, tread rubber, processes, production standards and training, all from Bandag. The appeal to the dealers was three-fold: One, they could have a turn-key manufacturing operation from a supportive, single-source supplier for a relatively small capital investment; two, they could retread virtually any size tire — from tires on forklifts to those on road graders — with one basic system; and, three, they could make money producing and selling quality Bandag® retreads (along with new tires made by other companies) as their own local or regional market demanded.

'rank Nelson and
{on Seiler, two of
3andag's first and
nost respected
employees, apply
ushion to a buffed
ndustrial tire casing.

Les Thompson, an early Bandag retread technician, shows the step-by-step process that launched the industry's best system.

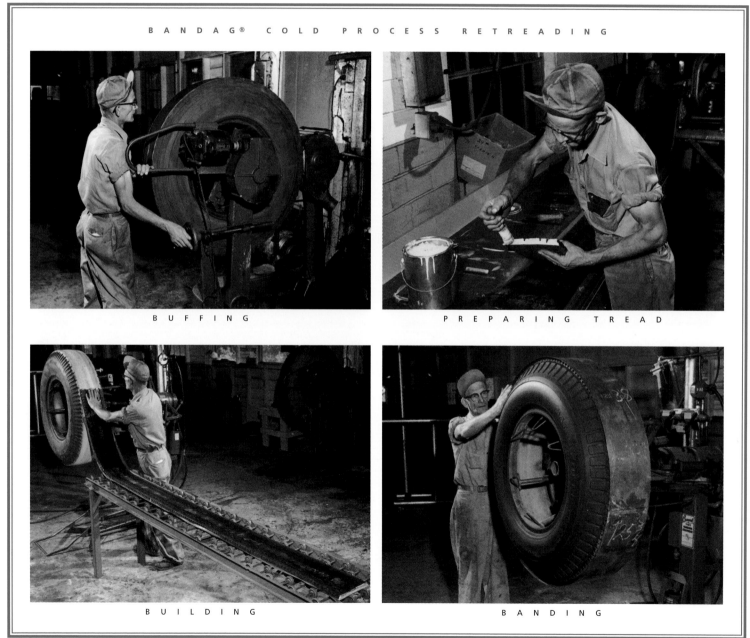

B A N D A G® C O L D P R O C E S S R E T R E A D I N G

B U F F I N G

P R E P A R I N G T R E A D

B U I L D I N G

B A N D I N G

B A N D A G® C O L D P R O C E S S R E T R E A D I N G

R I M I N S E R T I O N

B O N D I N G

F I N I S H E D T I R E

Howells Tire Service in Pottsville, Pennsylvania, became a Bandag dealership in 1958. In 1993, as they celebrated 35 years as a Bandag dealer, the business was run by a grandson, a third generation of Howells.

Roy (fourth from left) and his team used the company plane to visit many dealers. This Bandag dealer visit was with Stan Koziara (center wearing hat) of Stan the Tire Man located in Mount Vernon, Illinois. Stan was a very successful and popular Bandag dealer in the '60s.

In one of the most crucial times in Bandag's early days, Carver had to sell franchises to dealers to generate capital and do it in a hurry. In January 1961, persistent problems in the cold capping process, investment in major equipment and the unreliability of the early product had left Bandag technically bankrupt. It was do or die. So, Carver hopped into his plane and flew around to seven dealers with whom he had partnered, raising $50,000 over a long weekend. Martin Carver likes to say, "If the weather had been bad that weekend, Bandag wouldn't be here today." That trip was symbolic of the literally fly-by-the-seat-of-the-pants style that characterized Bandag's entrepreneurial operation in those early years.

Bandag needed a more aggressive sales force. The next October after Carver's emergency fly-around, he hired Harold Vischer, who had 24 years of experience with Firestone, to be his chief sales person. Vischer says he was reluctant to take the job because he "heard the company was broke. I only planned to stay with Bandag a year, but because I didn't have a job at the time, I decided to give it a go." Vischer retired 17 years later.

Vischer says he and Carver "became the best of friends, though I never called him Roy." They frequently flew together in Carver's plane on company business. In fact, Vischer took flying lessons "so I could take the wheel if he had a heart attack."

Charley Marsha
Grismer Tire; Har
Beam, one of Bandag
premier salesme
and George Zimme
Bandag Nation
Accounts Sale
Manager examine
display of industri
press-ons at Grisme
Tire in Ohi

For Your Safety
Have Firestone
SEAT BELTS
INSTALLED TODAY
Just Say "CHARGE IT"
LET US ROTATE YOUR TIRES TODAY
GET MORE TIRE MILEAGE

*"The [dealer prospect] got stranded overnight because of the snow-storm. So we ended up buying him a razor and a new pair of underwear. Well, anyway, we signed him up."*
*– Harold Vischer*

"One time when the weather was really bad," recalls Vischer, now in his nineties, "we had to set the plane down in Dayton, Ohio. It was really snowing. Well, there was a prospect, you know, a potential dealer there, so Carver, he says, 'Let's get him over here for a meeting.' We did that, but this guy, he got stranded overnight because of the snowstorm. So, you know, we ended up buying him a razor and a new pair of underwear. Well, anyway, we signed him up."

Vischer reflected Carver's own intensity about business, and his natural sales ability won him a place in Bandag's "Hall of Fame." A year after Vischer was hired, Bandag brought on another experienced sales manager to handle U.S. sales so "Visch" could devote more time to overall sales strategies and international markets. The company had an additional five commissioned sales people by 1962.

Bandag's management team was able to visit dealers often with the addition of the corporate plane.

By 1963, with the new one-ply cushion gum, vastly improved equipment, and a highly driven sales force, Bandag began to roll. Having nothing to lose, Bandag proclaimed its retreads could run twice as long as the hot cappers,' advertising with the slogan "Double the Mileage Guaranteed." By that time the Bandag® retread really was a superior product, and the aggressive marketing worked.

By the mid-1960s, Bandag was making real money, rapidly growing, supporting its dealer network and earning a reputation as the pre-cured retread industry leader.

Bandag not only left the hot cappers in the dust, but the Bandag process ultimately challenged new-tire companies as well. Before Bandag came along, truck companies used recaps sparingly, primarily on trailers.

"Stan the Tire Man" was a successful tire store chain and Bandag dealer in the Midwest. It was also a moniker for Stan Koziara, its owner, who was inducted into the TIA (Tire Industry Association) Hall of Fame in 1987. Stan had a retread shop in Mt Vernon, Illinois and a few tire stores throughout central Illinois. This was a classic store front in Salem, Illinois complete with muffler man and Uniroyal gal.

In the '60s the pressure chamber was added to the equipment line. Destined to eventually replace the bonding room, the pressure chamber used air pressure and electric heat to more effectively bond Bandag tread rubber to the casing. Although it was a tremendous addition to the equipment line it did present some challenges to deliver.

But, when they saw that reliable Bandag® retreads could extend tire life on both tractors and trailers, with huge savings, they bought fewer new tires. Of course, the new tire companies like Goodyear and Uniroyal campaigned against Bandag® retreads in various ways, but Bandag's innovative marketing, including "wild and wacky" product demonstrations, eventually persuaded the trucking industry that Bandag® retreads were as reliable as new tires, maybe even more so.

As the early Bandag employees had envisioned, the Bandag pre-cured, cold-cap process not only raised the standards of the formerly fragmented retread industry but revolutionized American tire production, sales and distribution. In many ways, those "bastards of the tire industry" had changed the world.

Plant 3 opens on Muscatine's South end. (left to right): Harold "Hoz" Vischer, Jr., Jerry Baillie, Ray Stratton, Frank Nelson, Harold Vischer, Wally Hickey and George Zimmer.

Bandag® retreads have successfully passed Federal Aviation Agency requirements. Here Ed Brodie and Roger Cleffman examine an airline test wheel.

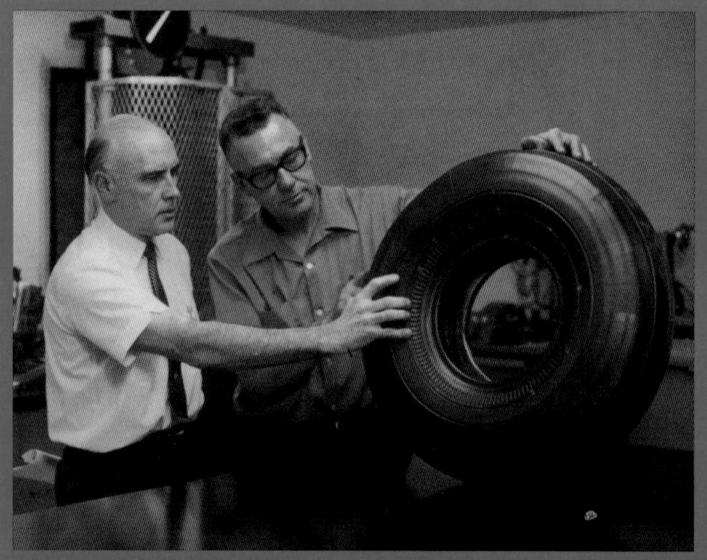

Ed Kopf, a retread technician, checks the balance of an aircraft tire. At one time Bandag supplied retreads to over 60 aircraft accounts, including two types of high speed jet fighter tires for the U.S. Navy.

Charles Edwards was Vice President of Manufacturing, Domestic & Foreign in 1969. Later in his career he assumed the role of President.

Gene Seyb, Vice President, Finance, and John McMullan, Director of Materials, examine Bandag's new NCR Century 100 computer. The installation of this computer, in 1969, is another example of Bandag's commitment to leading the industry. (In 1977 Seyb was promoted to President.)

At a typical industry trade show, Bandag highlights industrial tire products and the equipment utilized to create them.

Industrial tires, both pneumatic and solid, represented a major retreading opportunity for Bandag. Many major companies used fork lift trucks, cargo pullers and other warehouse equipment to move products to trucks for shipping.

Overstated perhaps? Well, you've heard this: "For want of a shoe, the horse was lost, for want of a horse the rider was lost, for want of a rider the battle was lost." Here's the update: "For want of a tire, a truck was lost, for want of a truck, the product was lost, for want of a product, prosperity was lost." Carver's original vision not only made him and early Bandag stockholders very wealthy, but Bandag® retreads improved the business of trucking itself.

Fifty years after Bandag got its start amidst the cornfields of Iowa, the economy of the United States and other countries, too, owes a major debt to trucks outfitted with cost-effective Bandag® retreads, delivering millions of products — with a minimum of downtime — over billions of miles. ▪

This advertising poster promoted the fact Bandag® retreads not only extend the useful life of the tire, but in many cases they outperform new tires in mileage performance and wear.

Jack Limbaugh of Jack's OK Tire Service gave a Bandag testimonial in this 1960s ad. Like many Bandag dealers, Jack enjoyed the life and built his business close to home, which was Algona, Iowa.

ROY CARVER — BIOGRAPHY

*Bandag's Founder Still Its Inspiration*

## Turning Lemons into Lemonade

You don't walk very far into Bandag's headquarters before seeing larger-than-life images of the founder, Roy J. Carver, and you don't talk to long-time employees more than a few minutes before hearing a Carver story or two.

Although Roy Carver died of a heart attack in 1981 and hadn't really managed the company for a decade before that, he remains a larger-than-life presence at Bandag today. It's as though employees glance over their shoulders every so often to see if he approves.

There are all sorts of stories. Some deal with his legendary intelligence, going back to his childhood. Roy was a troublemaker at school and seemed incapable of learning. However, his eighth grade teacher realized his potential, took an interest in him and suggested he get his tonsils and adenoids out. Sure enough, as she suspected, he was a very bright child with a hearing problem.

Very bright. She recounted when a traveling salesman, known to be an expert checkers player, came to town. Young Roy whipped him soundly, and when the man asked how he learned to play so well, the boy said, "I taught myself."

Some tales capture his derring-do. When he was a boy growing up in tiny Preemption, Illinois, he liked to hop a freight train from time to time just to see what was around the bend. One time a red-faced conductor caught him but let him stay on the strength of Roy's promise that he'd pay for the fare later, which he did. Moral of that story: Carver's word was his bond, but he didn't always play by other people's rules.

*"Carver was one of the reasons I wanted to be part of this company. I tried to pay him back by being loyal and honest, and doing the job as well as I could."*
*— Herb Roelle*

At 6'5" tall and always impeccably dressed, Roy Carver had a larger-than-life presence.

*"A real entrepreneur sees the world differently from most of us. Somehow he or she has a different trigger for curiosity. An entrepreneur like Roy Carver lives in a perpetual world of 'what if.'"*
*— Bill Block*

Nowak (Center) prepares a toast in celebration of Bandag's next big milestone.

Years later, former Muscatine Mayor Evelyn Schauland made the same point: "He was picked up for speeding many times. He wouldn't stop for stop signs. He never waved. He had places to go, and he did."

Several stories mention his aeronautical exploits, including flying his plane in a loop-de-loop under the old Muscatine High Bridge, and his solo flight in 1954 in a single-engine Beachcraft Bonanza — with extra gas tanks in the passenger compartment — across the Atlantic to Europe. The *Cedar Rapids Gazette* reported: "He was so impatient he sometimes landed his jet out of turn at airports. He once set his helicopter down smack in the middle of Venice, Italy. He flew the Atlantic in an ice storm. His passengers usually had white knuckles."

Flying was more than a hobby for Roy Carver, enabling him to travel the globe in search of opportunities and people that would make his companies a success. He had started pursuing it in earnest during World War II when airplane fuel wasn't rationed. Being able to fly gave him a world vision for his companies and products, and gave the Carver Pump Co., Carver Foundry Products and later Bandag a significant competitive advantage.

He was a big man — six feet, five inches tall — and his equally big vision enabled him to parlay a $100,000 investment in Bandag into a tall fortune estimated at $300 million. Forbes magazine once described him as "a big burly man with a pussycat touch who makes strong allies of his employees — a man with the Midas touch who knows a good deal when he sees one." Ed Kopf, a long-time employee, remembers, "We treasured the drive Mr. Carver had. When he set his mind to what he wanted, he could get people behind him."

Of all the stories, though, perhaps the one closest to a corporate metaphor — capturing the spirit of both the man and his company — is the little anecdote told by Harold Vischer, Bandag's long-time vice president of sales.

"Once we were having lunch in this ritzy hotel in Lagos, Nigeria, when Carver orders a lemonade. They bring him something else, a reconstituted lemon drink or something," Vischer recalls with a chuckle. "Carver doesn't like it, so he calls this waiter over, you see, and tells him to bring a big pitcher of ice water and some lemons and sugar. When he gets all the stuff he needs — right there in that fancy dining room with all its silver and linen tablecloths — Carver stirs all of us up some lemonade."

This story says a lot about the Carver personality, which over the years Bandag has turned into an implicit corporate credo.

First, consider the setting — Lagos, Nigeria. The farm boy from Preemption, Illinois, representing a company in Muscatine, Iowa, just happens to be having a business lunch in Lagos, Nigeria. Carver and Bandag were players on the world scene from the beginning, and you can't appreciate how the company grew so dramatically until you take into account the company's excursions all over the earth, a reflection of Carver's own wanderlust. When Bandag advertised for executives, it promised them they could travel and see the world, and they had to.

Second, Carver never settled for reconstituted anything. He wanted the pure, natural and original. For example, while retread processes that preceded Bandag often used unreliable reclaimed rubber, Carver was determined to produce as pure and high quality rubber tread as possible. "I never wanted to make money off a lousy product," Carver often said. Excellence has always been a hallmark of Bandag.

*"He was picked up for speeding many times. He wouldn't stop for stop signs. He never waved. He had places to go, and he did."*
*— Evelyn Schauland*

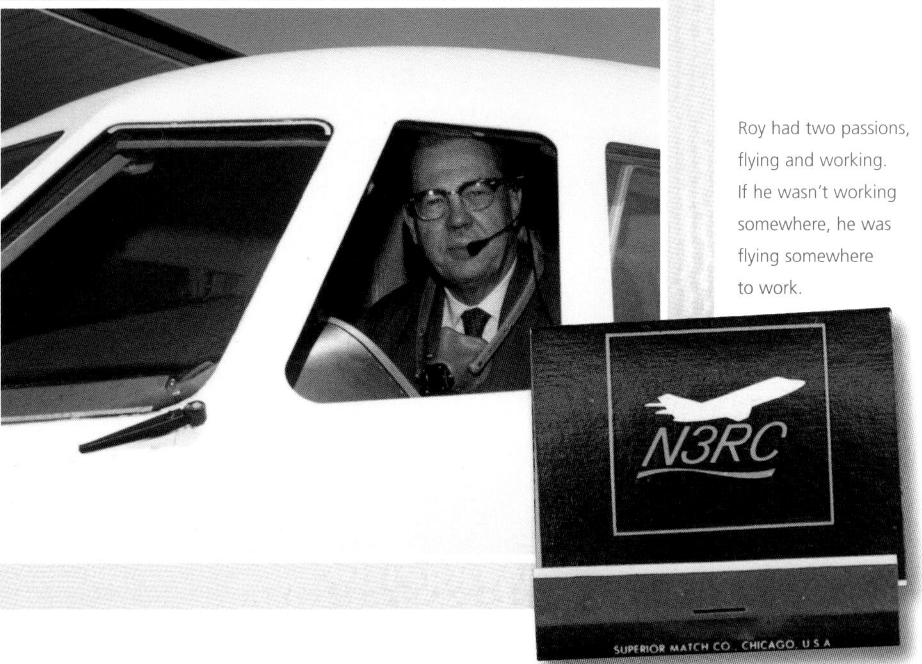


Roy had two passions, flying and working. If he wasn't working somewhere, he was flying somewhere to work.

Roy is presented with the Man of the Year award by the Quint City B'Nai B'Rith in 1974 for his community service.

Bill Block, head of corporate communications, notes, "Not only Bandag but everything Carver put his hand to had to be the best. His pumps, for example, were best in class, and that quality netted many lucrative contracts."

Third, the story illustrates that, when Carver knew what he wanted, he didn't hesitate to go get the ingredients and keep stirring the pitcher until things tasted right. The Bandag retreading process struck plenty of people as a sour idea when Carver introduced it — several thought he had been scammed by Nowak — but he kept stirring until Bandag got it right. The ingredients included the versatility to sell and supply worldwide, so — to do business in foreign countries without being at a disadvantage — Carver became fluent in Spanish, French and German. His friend Harold Vischer says Carver actually "knew five or six languages. He was a brain." Whether it was checkers or high-stakes business deals, Carver taught himself. Whatever it took.

At Carver's funeral, Iowa Gov. Robert Ray described him as "a unique man, a genius of sorts. He had the capability to dream and to fulfill dreams that were beyond the imaginations of most people. He had a knack of seeing opportunities, the drive and determination to succeed, and the creative and innovative ability to resolve inevitable problems."

Bill Block adds, "A real entrepreneur sees the world differently from most of us. Somehow he or she has a different trigger for curiosity. An entrepreneur like Roy Carver lives in a perpetual world of 'what if.'"

And, fourth, Roy Carver didn't really mind what people around him thought; he wasn't embarrassed by standing out in a crowd as a maverick, doing the boisterous, even the impolite, and certainly the unpredictable. Over the years he had his detractors. He didn't care.

Roy had even defied his father. The dismal years of the Great Depression had taken its toll on his father's Ford dealership, so it's not surprising Roy's dad thought his son was foolish when he wanted to start a pump factory in 1938.

But Roy managed to parlay his $100,000 investment into a profitable company, starting Carver Pump Co. in Matherville, Illinois. In the early 1950s, during a visit to Germany, Carver stumbled upon a new way to produce foundry products. He opened Carver Foundry Products in Muscatine in 1954.

That relentless refusal to concede defeat also carried Bandag early on. Recalled Herb Roelle, senior design engineer: "During those five or six really tough years, most businessmen would have given up. Mr. Carver never gave up. He just had a feeling in his bones that Bandag would succeed."

There's another lesson in the lemonade story, too. Roy Carver loved people, and he loved to entertain. The generosity and warmth that Carver shared with common folk as well as the rich and famous has been imitated thousands of times over by the way Bandag has treated dealers, employees and customers. His was an openness, free of racial, ethnic or nationalistic prejudice, and people around the world considered him a friend.

One biographer observed, "People were a fascination and a challenge for Roy Carver. During his life, he made close friendships with both the mighty and the humble throughout the world. He would talk economics with well-known politicians one minute and football and the weather with hotel maids the next."

John Kindschuh, vice president for administration at Augustana College, in Rock Island, Illinois, the recipient of a $1.5 million Carver gift, commented: "Whatever his wealth and capacity for flair, he had a strong sense of common touch." After Carver signed over the gift to Augustana, he went out for beers with some of the students. And he bought.

Roy loved people. He was equally at home with the factory line workers or hanging out with Gerald R. Ford (before he became U.S. President) and other celebrities.

Carver's sincere love of people certainly inspired his employees. His sales ace, Harold Vischer, says simply, "He was the best boss I ever worked for, and I worked for a few." Carver knew many of his employees even in later years by their first and last names. Roelle, who joined Bandag in 1959, recalled, "Carver was one of the reasons I wanted to be part of this company. I tried to pay him back by being loyal and honest, and doing the job as well as I could. Although Carver was like a bloodhound on the trail, he actually seemed to me to be an understanding and forgiving boss. He just wanted to make sure that you learned from your mistakes."

This 1979 Annual Report photo shows Carver with Pierre Debroux, President & Chief Executive Officer, and Gene Seyb, Vice Chairman of the Board.

Well, he wasn't all that forgiving of his managers, including Bandag presidents. As the Gazette reported: "Carver fired managers like he spent money. 'He was a very impulsive man,' said I.H. Petersen, former department store owner in Muscatine, and Carver's neighbor. 'When a (Bandag) president's time was up, he was done. He paid off their contracts like money was water.'"

Some of Carver's associates said his flamboyant nature interfered with his managing of Bandag, though they credited him with an uncanny ability to hire top-notch people. "He practically abdicated management to others," said one critic, "and that's what saved Bandag."

Gene Seyb, an executive who made it to retirement, remembered that Carver impulsiveness: "Sometimes Roy didn't know what he was going to do next. We'd be heading east on a business trip, in his jet, when all of a sudden over Indiana he'd bank to the south. 'Let's stop at New Orleans for dinner,' he'd say. Old Roy Carver. I liked the guy."

David Elderkin, Carver's long-time attorney, paid this tribute at Carver's death: "He had his critics, and some of the criticism is valid. But as Theodore Roosevelt once observed: 'It is not the critic who counts; not the man who points out how the strong man stumbled. The credit belongs to the man who is actually in the arena; whose face is marred by dust and sweat and blood; who strives valiantly; who errs and comes short again and again... who, at the best, knows the triumph of high achievement and who, at the worst, if he fails, at least fails while daring greatly.'"

Carver dared greatly and more often than not came out a winner. He loved life. In 1975, when he had already amassed a sizable fortune, he commented: "I don't worry about money any more. I worry about time — how much time do I have left? Everything I do is based on making as much of the day, the week, the month as I can."

More a rambunctious visionary than a typical businessman, Roy Carver nevertheless remains Bandag's inspiration. When people measure the company today as a worldwide corporation, or think about its future, many still do so against their perception of the standards of Roy Carver. Does this or that corporate decision or policy break new ground? Is it bold and truly innovative? Does it take into account the little guy as well as the bottom line?

All that's what Roy would expect. And what Bandag's new leadership embraces for the future. ▪

In March 1966, Bandag was awarded the President's "E" Award for excellence in expanding export markets. The company held an employee appreciation day in Muscatine and displayed the flag they could now fly. Left to right: Carver, Iowa Senator Jack Miller, Steven Keller, President and Harold Vischer Vice President of Sales.

This pin represented the award and was proudly displayed by Bandag executives. Bandag started in the export business in 1961.

bandag
bandag

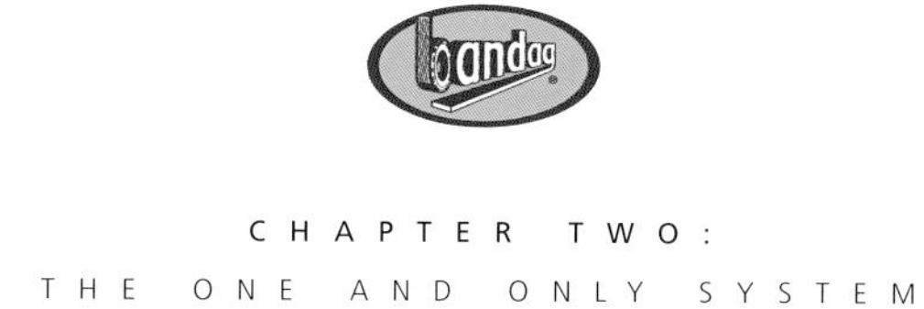




# SELLING THE WHOLE PACKAGE

*Roy Carver apparently had his Bandag franchise concept in mind from the beginning, establishing the first dealership barely six months after acquiring North American rights to the Bandag patents. What's so amazing about the Bandag dealership success story, though, is that Bandag sold franchisees for its production processes before those processes were perfected.*

*Roy Carver pulled this off largely on the power of his vision, personal charisma and ability to listen to dealers in the field. It didn't hurt either to have an equally tenacious sales person like Harold Vischer, who once commented, "I never had any problem getting sales."*

: the 1974 American
·tread Association
RA) trade show,
ft to right) Ron
ordon, Training
anager, Harold
scher, VP Sales and
arketing and Dan
llaghan, Marketing
anager look over a
w passenger tread
lder with an
A official.

Vischer, a very religious man, approached his work like a crusade. Martin Carver describes Vischer sallying forth "with a hunk of rubber in one hand and a Bible in the other." As one dealer recalled, "You couldn't waffle with Mr. Vischer. He'd say, 'OK, if you're not decisive enough to act on a great opportunity when it's staring you in the face, then you aren't decisive enough to be one of our dealers.' And he'd head for the door."

It was a tough sell in the early days, but Vischer — who once shot off a starter pistol to wake up his sales people after lunch — and his boss were up to the challenge.

It would have been one thing to develop an untested production process like Bandag's cold cap retread tire system, then sell and deliver quality retreads through a network of dealers. It would prove to be far more intimidating to franchise a complete vertically integrated production and marketing system, with all the equipment, raw materials, rigorous production standards, employee training, marketing materials and sales support. In the final analysis, Carver sold the idea by appealing to the same instinct that drove him — the lure of entrepreneurship.

*"So I took the plunge, even though a few people at Bandag told me I was taking a terrible risk. I just couldn't forget the idea that I wanted to be an entrepreneur like Roy Carver."*
*— Dan Callaghan*

With the Bandag franchise of the early years, says Twyla Hartman, franchise services specialist, "You could get an entire retread system for about $8,000, shop rags included." That meant people with small operations could get a turnkey, fully supported system for a relatively small investment, and they could, in effect, be manufacturers rather than simply selling what somebody else made, with the potential for far higher profits. It had a big appeal even to some Bandag employees with job security.

Dan Callaghan, now a principal of a successful Bandag dealership in Florida, got his first introduction to the company in 1969 when he was a 22-year-old Michelin trainee. He and his boss went to Muscatine to resolve a billing dispute, and Callaghan met Bandag employees Ron Seiler, Frank Nelson, Harold Vischer and others. "I started following Bandag's success because many of the dealers who sold new Michelin tires also sold Bandag retreads," Callaghan recalls.

"In 1970 I tried to get a Bandag franchise but couldn't swing it. Instead, I took a job with Bandag and moved from Chicago to Muscatine. I got promoted and was at a good level in the company, but I still desired to be an entrepreneur. I couldn't see myself playing corporate politics, and I had confidence in my ability to sell. So I took the plunge, even though a few people at Bandag told me I was taking a terrible risk. I just couldn't forget the idea that I wanted to be an entrepreneur like Roy Carver."

The Dan Callaghan family proudly displayed their Bandag dealership's 25th anniversary service award at the Bandag Business Conference in Rancho Mirage, California in 2002.

Following a somewhat similar path was Richard Newlon, who today runs Atlanta Tire Specialists out of a new 40,000-square-foot facility in Conyers, Georgia. He finished college and answered a Bandag ad promising he could travel and see the world. He got to do what the ad promised and along the way learned every phase of the Bandag operation under people like Frank Nelson and Ron Seiler. He ran a Bandag-owned dealership in Hong Kong, but "left the nest to become an entrepreneur" as an independent dealer in the late 1970s, starting with a partner in a 6,000-square-foot facility.

Perhaps the first impression you get when you visit his and other dealerships

Marvin Dice, of Dice Tire and Fay Wagner, Wagner Tire, display a stock certificate each had purchased to help the company through some lean times.

is that, as Newlon puts it, "this factory is as clean and light as a dentist's office." Newlon's is a sophisticated operation, staying current with the latest in Bandag computerized equipment, production training, certification and all the rest. "Right now we're turning out about 180 retreads a day." If you visited the place, you'd see the "one and only system" touted by Bandag marketing several years ago.

Today the equipment alone for an operation approaching that of Atlanta Tire Specialists probably would cost over a million dollars, estimates Twyla Hartman, not including the building to put it in and an adequate supply of tread rubber. "You're probably looking at $6 million or more to set up a major operation," she says.

Of course, the production equipment in the early days back in Plant 2 in Muscatine bore little resemblance to the high-tech operations today. It could be dangerous back then, as tires would explode under pressure, fires would start, and failures and frustrations were commonplace. But as Bandag research and development worked out the kinks, Bandag shared its knowledge and shipped its equipment to all parts of the world.

As Bandag got past the first years of trial and error, and gained the reputation as the quality retreader, dealers were eager to take advantage of Bandag's competitive footprint. Bandag not only sold the dealers on the quality but worked hard to help sell the product itself to the truckers. They would explain the "one and only system" to the drivers and fleet managers, then demonstrate tread toughness and cost savings. In many cases, it wasn't a matter of dealers pushing Bandag® retreads as much as truckers demanding them.

Marvin Bozarth, for many years executive director of the American Retreader Association, says: "Several people we knew were taking on Bandag franchises, and one of the big reasons was quality. Bandag was recognized for producing tires that got good mileage, for supplying training

and support for dealer personnel, and for generally insisting on high standards when the rest of the industry didn't have such high standards."

And, Bozarth says, Bandag was the dominant presence at the trade shows, demonstrating the latest technology, showing off new tread designs. "And, of course, when radial tires came along, Bandag's pre-cured process was superior." Dealers and truckers alike were impressed.

Selling the franchise to a dealer was one challenge, keeping him happy another. Gary Carlson, former president of the Muscatine Chamber of Commerce, who previously handled a lot of different Bandag management responsibilities over the years, says that the key was constant attention to supporting the dealers in more than superficial ways. "We understood that we needed to have 'great' dealers, so we worked closely with them, helping them keep an eye on the needs of the end user."

Bandag displayed at a few national shows such as this NTDRA trade show in the early '70s.

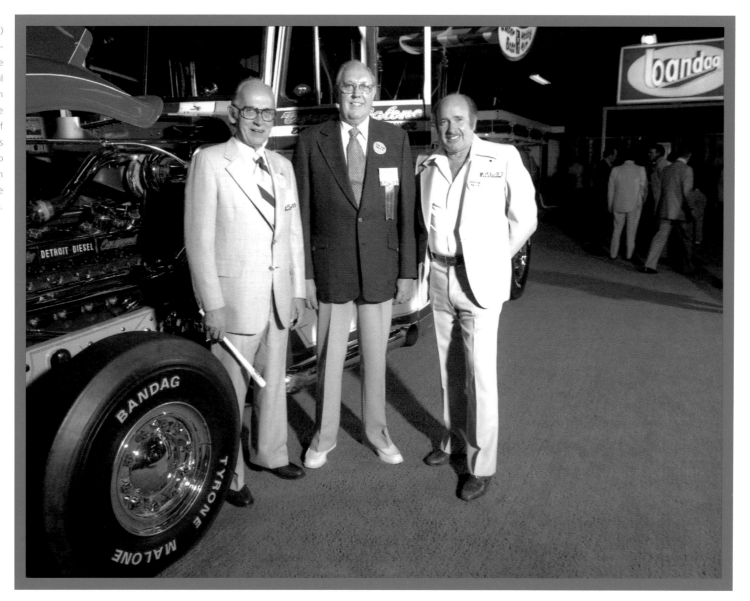


Harold Vischer (left) and Bandag spokesman Tyrone Malone (right) pose with Paul Clark at the ARA in 1978 next to the Super Boss, one of several vehicles Malone took to shows and on tour to promote Bandag® retreads.

*"Bandag was recognized for producing tires that got good mileage, for supplying training and support of dealer personnel, and for generally insisting on high standards when the rest of the industry didn't have such high standards."*
*— Marvin Bozarth*

*"[In the early days] you could get our entire retreading system for about $8,000, shop rags included."*
— *Twyla Hartman*

Ron Gordon (left) and Jerry Baillie (right) of Bandag's Training Department congratulate Sidney Katz and Jim Furlong of Merchant Tire Company. Furlong was the 10,000th trainee to successfully complete Bandag training class.

Bandag didn't just sell the franchise, ship the equipment and tread rubber, drop off some marketing materials, and send a Christmas card. Instead, the company truly partnered with the dealers across the entire operation to the satisfaction of the truckers and fleet managers whose livelihoods depended on those tires. Two-way communication and collaboration were critical to success.

To add some real excitement to the 1977 Bandag Dealer Business Conference, Bandag hired these two young men to drive this Bandag® retread-equipped Volkswagon Bus from Anchorage, Alaska to Rio De Janeiro. They arrived during the conference.

Harold Vischer says that there were seven key components to the partnership between Bandag and its dealers.

1. A complete sales program that helps make Bandag number one.
2. A complete advertising and promotional program that helps make Bandag number one.
3. A complete technical program that helps make Bandag number one.
4. A complete sales training program that helps make Bandag number one.
5. The best product in the retread industry.
6. The largest and best service engineering department with enough service engineers to be able to contact all Bandag dealers regularly.
7. The largest and best R&D group devoted exclusively to retreading and keeping the product number one.

The words Vischer chose like "complete," "number one," "largest" and "best" all speak of high standards of leadership. And Bandag employees have always tried to live in a world where those standards are consistently applied.

Back in Vischer's era, F. William Jung, then vice president of sales and marketing, said, "Our primary responsibility is to work along with the dealer in carrying out his business in all areas." With regard to advertising, Jim Lemkau, former director of advertising, noted that, "We provide all point-of-purchase aids for the dealer, including film cassette units, brochures, selling tools and personnel identification." Bandag also offered an all-encompassing co-op advertising program, prepared newspaper and magazine ad slicks, TV and radio spots and Yellow Page ads. "We also coordinate all trade show activity, incentive trips, international business conferences and regional sales meetings."

"The best hot cap I ever ran across couldn't compare to a Bandag."

"We used to have ten times as many flats before we switched to Bandags."

BANDAG SAFE ZONE | UP TO 75% LOSS | OVER 75% LOSS | UP TO TOTAL LOSS

160° 210° 260° 310° 360°

Curing is done at low temperatures, allowing your tire to retain full strength. No hot cap heat to age your tire body. You are insured of a longer running, better balanced tire for smoother riding.

bandag

Why the bandag retread is different.

"I get more miles out of Bandags than I do out of new tires. They're the best caps I've ever run."

bandag

cold process retreading delivers

AMERICA REDISCOVERS THE RETREAD

AND THE LATEST WORD IN RETREADS IS...

PATENTED COLD PROCESS RETREADING

bandag LOWERS DOWNTIME

Bandag introduces 3 tough new retreads to cut tire costs for light trucks and RV's.

Bandag advertisements and literature set the stage for Bandag sales calls.

As Bandag grew the company recognized the need for a special training program that would bring new dealers and their employees to Muscatine for intensified on-the-job training. The Bandag Training Institute was built in 1976 to take care of this need.

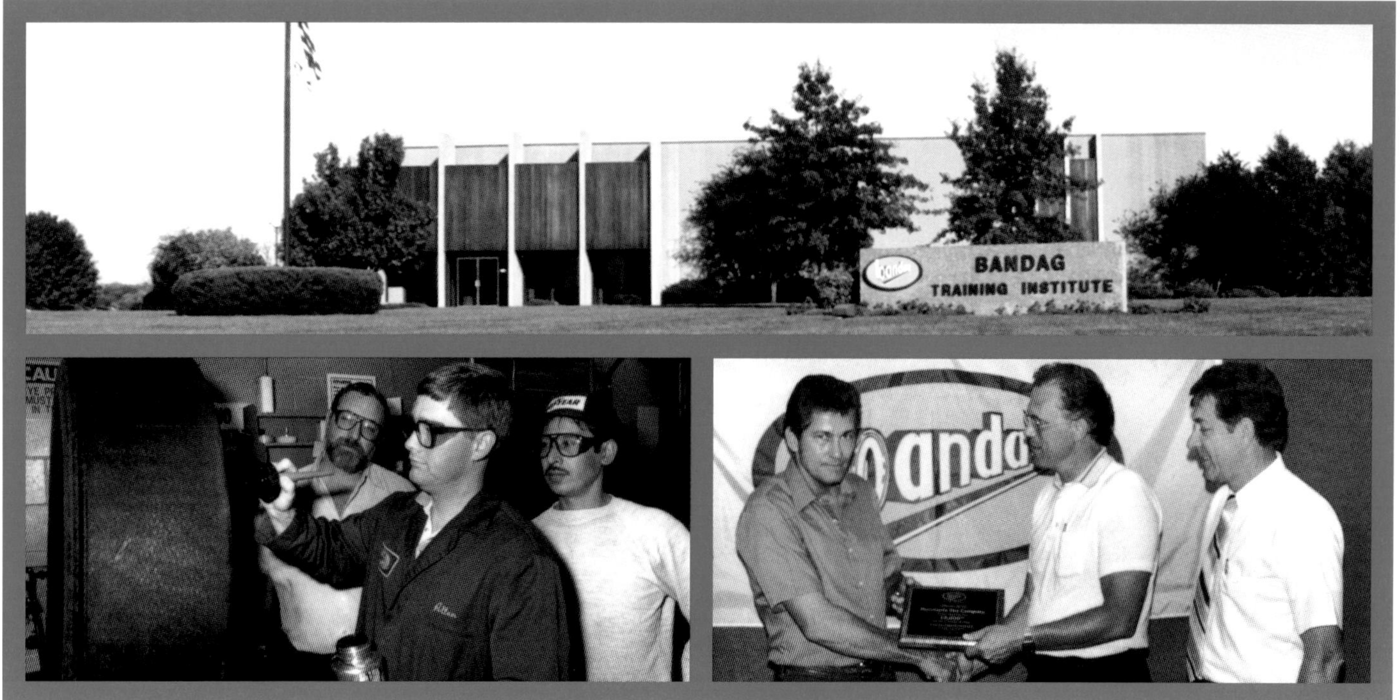


Bob Cowan receives a plaque recognizing him as the 15,000th graduate of the Bandag Training Institute. Presenting the plaque are Bandag Technical Trainer Dale Lovstad and Walt Luethy, Technical Trainer Manager.

Bandag has long boasted the finest training in the retread industry, with a technical training center opened in 1976 and a new Learning Center in 1999. "The courses would put some college curricula to shame," according to one assessment. Each course of study was based on the principle that training properly conducted would pay for itself. Ron Gordon, a vice president for training in the '70s, said: "We believe that, if the dealer's employees know more about retreading, they'll produce and sell more retreads. This means we'll sell more rubber… a situation we feel is highly desirable at both the manufacturing and dealer level."

In 1997, in its 40th anniversary year, Bandag offered 243 technical classes (26 courses) with 2,077 attendees along with a core curriculum of 148 classes (16 courses) with 2,886 attendees.

This shop manual was commonly referred to as the "Bandag bible."

Dick O'Brien, Mayor of Muscatine, Martin Carver and Suzanne Miller, Vice President of Training dig the first shovel of dirt for the new Bandag training facility.

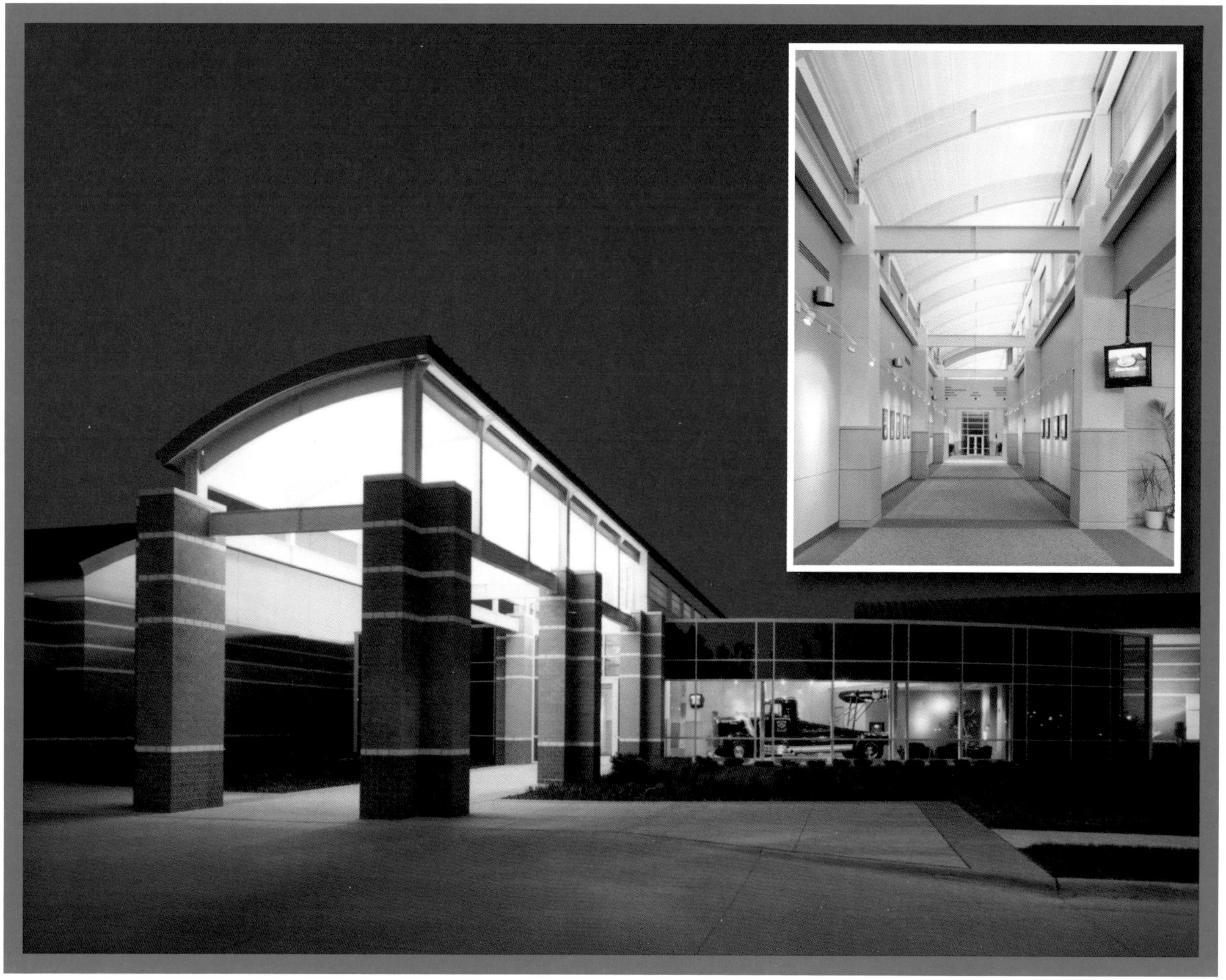

This wonderful facility includes a library, a state-of-the-art retread shop, employee offices, a series of both large and small classrooms, a kitchen and an auditorium-like space that can be used for very large groups.

Bandag Service Engineers are trained to help dealers solve equipment and production problems in the field with a visit to the dealership or a phone call from the help desk.

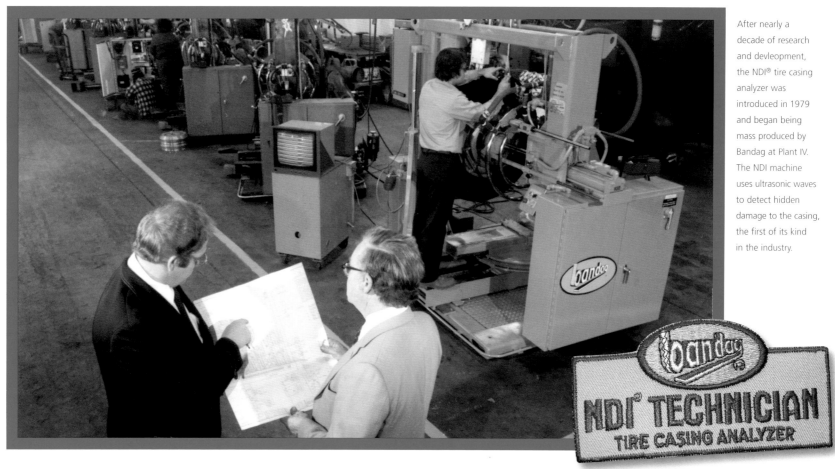


After nearly a decade of research and devleopment, the NDI® tire casing analyzer was introduced in 1979 and began being mass produced by Bandag at Plant IV. The NDI machine uses ultrasonic waves to detect hidden damage to the casing, the first of its kind in the industry.

Other key components of dealer support are product development and service engineering. Robert Koegler, a former senior vice president, group marketing, said: "We don't experience many difficulties because we leave nothing to chance. The ultimate goal of each service engineer at Bandag is to make certain every system sold is properly installed, maintained and utilized through a program of service and industrial engineering follow-up. And this Bandag does," he asserted, "with more perseverance than any other company in the retread industry."

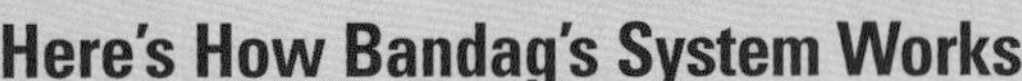

## Here's How Bandag's System Works

While not every dealer has the latest equipment, here's the basic Bandag process which is the foundation of Bandag's success for 50 years.

The used tire receives a visual, hands-on, seven-step inspection from bead-to-bead, inside and out, to determine the casing's suitability for retreading. All visible and known injuries are identified and marked during initial inspection. Next is an electronic inspection utilizing the NDT®-II B™ to uncover any "through the tire" penetrations in the casing not visible during initial inspection. The next inspection step is to scan the tire with the 7400 *INSIGHT*® Casing Analyzer, which uses shearographic inspection technology to uncover any hidden casing defects. Shearography utilizes laser technology to optically dissect the casing while a camera captures the images at varying vacuum pressures applied to the casing. The vacuum pressures provide stresses to separated components and movement is displayed through video exposing the casing anomalies. The casing inspections combined with the casing condition, age and fleet specifications are evaluated to determine the casing's suitability for retreading to assure a high quality product.

A tire making the grade moves to the buffing process (a lathe-like process) where the 8400 Automated Buffer is utilized to true up the casing and remove remaining tread design and prepare the worn surface for accepting a new tread. Injuries identified during the inspection process and at buffing are removed or "skived" away from the casing. These injuries are then replaced with structurally sound materials to restore the original integrity of the casing.

The tire then moves to the 6400 Extruder. In a one-step process, a layer of bonding rubber, called cushion, is extruded onto the prepared casing surface. All skives are filled and the shoulders are stripped, preparing the casing for its new tread. The building process applies the new high quality Bandag tread straight and centered onto the casing. The 5400 OSM™ Builder allows the dealer to match the tread design at the splice for the ultimate in retread appearance.

Next the 1240 Envelope Spreader is used to install a flexible rubber envelope around the casing which is secured to the tire with the Bandag patented rubber ARC® Ring System. The integrity of the curing assembly is checked and the tire is now ready for curing. The Model 4150 Chamber is used to cure the assembly so that the tread is permanently attached to the casing by applying heat and pressure to the uncured bonding layer for a specified amount of time. The 4150 Chamber is designed to cure 22 tires during the same cure cycle. A final visual and hands-on inspection bead-to-bead, inside and out, assures that the tire is ready to go back on the road again.

The system is highly efficient, and the dirty, worn tire at the beginning comes through at the end looking — and more importantly running — like a new tire. ▪

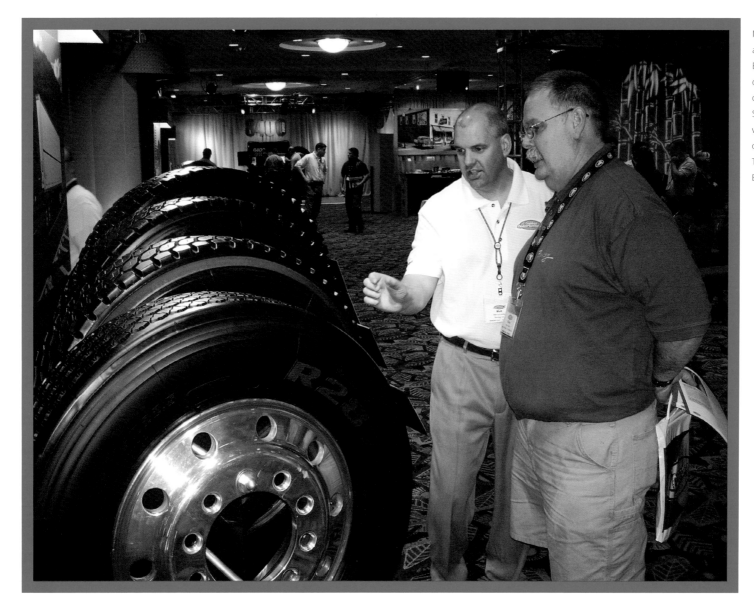


Matt Schnedler, a second generation Bandag employee, dicusses the benefits of Bandag's Application Specific tread designs with Rick Holden of Bain & Holden Tire Company, Inc., Englewood, Tennessee.

Throughout its phenomenal growth, Bandag always asserted it was the best of breed and constantly getting better. The original promise to potential dealers was pretty much the same as today. You'll read things like this in materials marketing the franchise: "Bandag is the world leader in retread technology with training, service and systems-support to match. We're a single-source supplier dedicated to providing you the highest profit return on your equipment investments...."

As it was in the days of Roy Carver, the fundamental appeal is still to those with his kind of spirit: "Bandag is committed to the ideals of independent business people. That's why so many Bandag franchise owners are independent family businesses. That entrepreneurial spirit is key to the strength of the Bandag brand." ▪

According to the Lee Way fleet's tire buyer, Jim Gay, "Early in 1958 I sent four casings to Muscatine. When we got them back we put them on a tractor making the Oklahoma City/Amarillo run, the roughest we had at that time. In three months, those tires had logged 50,000 miles. That was already more than we had been getting from our hotcaps. Within a year we had sent 400 tires to Muscatine."

## Hot Capping? Bandag Proved It Not So Hot

The retread process Roy Carver brought back to Muscatine, Iowa, with its original patents was anything but fully developed, and the early days were fraught with problems. Trucks would literally drive off their Bandag® retreads, leaving tread rubber strips on the pavement.

Still, Carver persevered, wagering the resources of his Carver Pump Co. to refine the Bandag process in the face of more than a little ridicule. He was convinced the Bandag way would prove superior to the one prevailing in the U.S. tire industry.

Truck tires in the 1960s were nearly all bias-ply tires, and technology in rubber compounding was primitive by 21st century standards. The "experts" said it was impossible to attach two pieces of cured rubber — the tread and the casing — with a bond strong enough to keep them from separating under road conditions. Instead, traditional retreading involved applying a rubber compound called a camelback to a tire casing, then placing it into a mold where the new rubber is vulcanized to the casing while simultaneously molding in a tread design. It's called hot capping.

Carver disagreed with the experts, seeing the flaws in what the rest of the industry was doing. High temperature and pressure were necessary to achieve the vulcanizing and molded tread, but too much heat and pressure could fatigue and shorten the life of the original bias ply tire casing. Therein lay the rub: Apply enough heat and pressure to vulcanize the tread to the casing, and make it tough enough for satisfactory wear, and the life of the casing may be shortened. Not enough heat and pressure, and the tread may peel off or come out of the mold so under-cured it quickly wears out.

With the Bandag approach, a strip of incredibly tough tread rubber is molded to the correct width and design in a factory press, apart from the tire casing. Because the tire casing isn't involved at this stage, high heat and pressure can be used to mold treads even longer wearing than those of some new tires. These dense, rugged treads, in a variety of designs for varied applications, deliver more mileage with fewer punctures. The dramatic cost savings occurs when sound, undamaged casings can be retreaded again and again.

The challenges Carver and his colleagues faced in the early days involved developing a bonding material and method that would vulcanize at temperatures low enough not to shorten the life of the casing and still hold the tread to the tire. With engineering breakthroughs involving flexible envelope curing and one-ply cushion gum, the problems were resolved. With patents on those aspects of the process, Bandag was ready to roll, and at that point there was no serious competition. ▪

In 1979 Bandag launched a new tread rubber compound named EL-80.™ The name refers to the "Extended Life" the compound will give Bandag retreads produced throughout the 1980s. Bandag's vice president of research and development, Ed Brodie (right), and Charles Edwards display the EL-80 ad campaign that would appear in trade magazines.

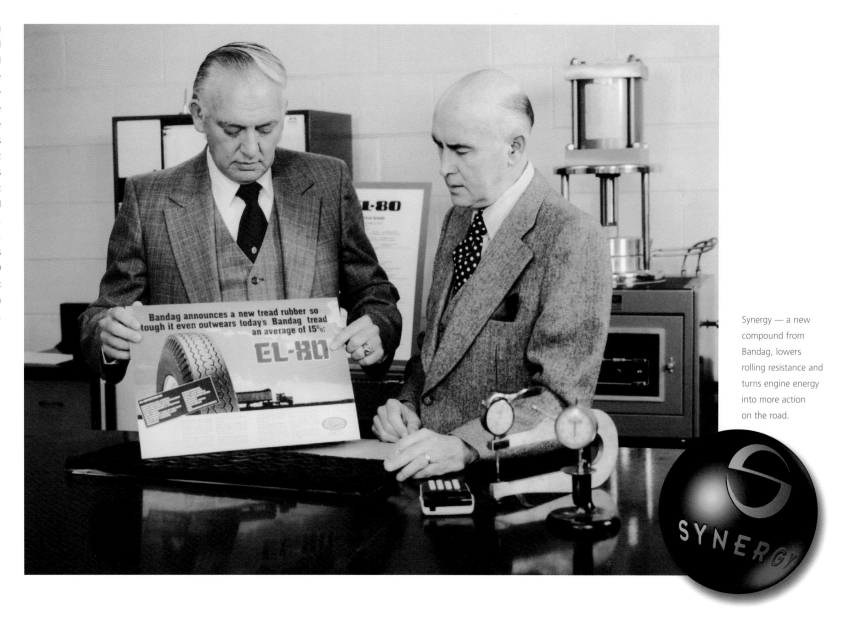

Synergy — a new compound from Bandag, lowers rolling resistance and turns engine energy into more action on the road.

## Talking About Their Dad

On the eve of Bandag's 50th anniversary, three of Roy Carver's sons, Martin, Roy, Jr., and John sat down to reflect on their father's personality and accomplishments.

Roy Carver's four sons, (clockwise from left): Martin, John, Clayton, and Roy Jr.

Martin: "Like our dad, Bandag was a different sort; we marched to a different beat. We never considered ourselves a mainstream business. For one thing, Dad had a sense of quality long before (W. Edwards) Demming made it the emphasis in the business world. Dad would read somebody the riot act if they didn't give their best. He also had a real sense of destiny. Once he was offered five million dollars for the company — some of us thought he should take it — but he just laughed."

John: "He could be difficult as a manager, but he had a knack for surrounding himself with outstanding people. Dad could get people to do things very few others could. But he didn't have much respect for people who wouldn't put it all on the line, wouldn't take risks the way he did. It was very important for him to work hard and be successful."

Roy, Jr.: "He had a riverboat gambler's sense of risk taking. For instance, he'd fly his plane, estimating his fuel consumption with a slide rule. There were people in the company who vowed never to fly with him; they'd always go commercial. I can remember he called me to shine my car lights on the air strip so he could find his way in during a thunderstorm. He was one of those people born with the eye of the tiger, ferocity about accomplishing things."

When you listen to Carver's sons, you know they're proud of their dad. ▪

## Carver Scammed, Estate Collects

Perhaps the most embarrassing point of Roy Carver's life was the realization he had been taken in an Arab oil scam.

Among the guests on board the Carver yacht in the Mediterranean one evening in 1975 was an official of Sedco Industrial Corp. of Dallas, reportedly the world's largest oil-drilling firm. According to the *Des Moines Register*, the Texan persuaded Carver to invest $2.5 million to reactivate abandoned oil wells in the Persian Gulf. But first Carver had to pay an Arab official to get a drilling permit. The permit cost $1.5 million.

"The oil was there, all right, but unusable. It was contaminated with deadly hydrogen sulfide gas that would have been too expensive to remove," the *Register* reported. Carver sued Sedco for $17 million. In 1981 a U.S. District Court judge ruled that Carver's permit payment was "influence money" and illegal, but also found that Sedco had known from the beginning the oil was polluted. Carver was awarded $13.2 million, and accumulated interest took the amount to $19.5 million.

"Carver did not live to collect the award. He died at 71 while at dinner in Marbella, Spain, in June 1981 — two months before the (judge's) decision," the *Register* noted. "The oil lawsuit money went into his estate." ▪

## Carver Philosophy Produced Champions

Roy Carver had been a wrestler in high school and college, and he took an extraordinary interest in the University of Iowa's legendary wrestling program under head coach Olympian Dan Gable.

Carver knew all the wrestling moves and seldom missed a meet. If he couldn't attend, he would have his secretary do so, and she would phone him with the results no matter where he was in the world.

"Mr. Carver was a great inspiration to our program by introducing the 'conceive, believe, achieve' philosophy to young wrestlers," Coach Gable said. Recruits were told they must "think" they could be champions, "know" they had the ability to win and "reach" their goal through relentless effort.

It was the same philosophy that permeated the ranks of Bandag, including those of successful dealerships, who used not just Bandag processes, supplies and equipment but also the Carver commitment to excellence to win big in their marketplace. ▪

## Do You Know How to Bale Hay?

Roy Carver had a strong work ethic and in the early days he loved to hire "farm boys," who like himself had grown up knowing the value of hard labor.

"One of the reasons for that," says Ron Seiler, "is he was having trouble keeping boys from town on the job. He worked them too hard."

Maybe that's why Ed Kopf worked at Bandag for 40 years. He remembers when he went to Carver looking for a job. "Did you grow up on a farm?" Carver asked. "Yes, sir," Kopf answered. "Yeah," Carver said, "but do you know how to bale hay?" ▪

## Bandag Fueled Carver's Remarkable Philanthropy

Roy Carver's generosity was part of his nature, but thousands of Bandag employees can take pride in the fact that Carver's philanthropy was made possible by their good work.

Although the Iowa millionaire was viewed by many in his state as a free-wheeling jetsetter, he donated millions to education and other causes. His gifts to the University of Iowa alone amounted to nearly $10 million. Other gifts to area colleges and universities included $1.5 million to Augustana College, Rock Island, for construction of the Roy J. Carver Physical Education Center, and $750,000 to the University of Northern Iowa, Cedar Falls, to help initiate construction of a mini-dome coliseum.

Carver, a fine arts expert, gave the Davenport, Iowa, Art Gallery a rare 17th century oil painting by a Dutch master. He also donated $200,000 to help fund a swim center at Muscatine High School.

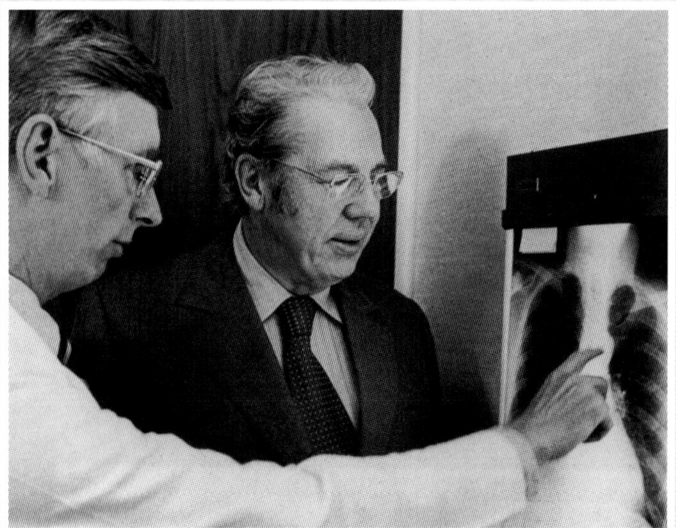

Roy tours the University of Iowa Hospital, a frequent recipient of his philanthropic generosity.

In 1971 he provided his first major gift to the University of Iowa — $3.5 million for scholarships, professorships, furnishing at Hancher Auditorium, an addition to the art museum, and artificial turf for the football stadium. In 1974 Carver gave the University of Iowa another $3.7 million, the largest individual gift in the school's history. More than half of the amount, $2 million, was allocated for construction of a major addition to the University Hospitals and Clinics. The addition, known as Carver Pavilion, houses a trauma and emergency treatment center.

Employees working in the sweaty Bandag factories of the early years probably didn't think their diligence in implementing Roy Carver's commitment to excellence would have implications for Iowa sports, education and healthcare benefiting thousands in Iowa and elsewhere. But that's how things worked out. ▪

F
TAN
TANDY CORP.
+00
HTN
HOUGHTON MIFFLIN
+00
GPO
NEM
NEWMONT MINING
−00
NEM PR A
−000
WRI
WACHOVIA REALTY INVESTMENTS
+0C
LUD
BDG
BANDAG, INC.
+65
CGG
CHIC. PNEUMATIC TOOL
−00
IBM
INT'L BUSINESS MACH.
−000
DG
ASSOCIATED DRY GOODS
SYMBOL
DC
DE CORDOVA

# THE DARLING OF WALL STREET

*Bandag, Incorporated, submitted its first public stock offering at $12 per share in 1968. Eleven months later the stock split three for one, in 1970 it split two for one, in 1973 again two for one, and in 1974 Bandag was listed on the "big board" of the New York Stock exchange. The company that began in a small Iowa town was now a big-time player in the world marketplace, and Bandag's explosive growth spurt would last for over two decades. It was amazing.*

Richard Howland of the New York Stock Exchange, (left), Bandag Chairman Roy Carver, and Bandag President Stephen Keller watch ticker tape projection (ticker symbol BDG) of the first sale of stock.

Warren Heidbreder, former chief financial officer, says the key to selling investors turned on Bandag's ability to develop and prove its business model. "Carver first had to figure out the underlying concept, then prove it could really work financially, then take it to market. There were lots of decisions to be made. For example, how do you price the product? The cost of the cushion gum was a key factor in the pricing, and that and other things were closely guarded secrets."

Actually, President Steve Keller is the man generally credited with putting the finishing touches on the business model and packaging it for sale on Wall Street.

Former Chairman and CEO Martin Carver says Keller "was a strong presence. He ran the business like he owned it, and he proved to be the right man for the time." And Keller, along with Roy Carver, Ed Brodie and Harold Vischer are in the Bandag "Hall of Fame."

"Once the economies of the process were sorted out," Heidbreder says, "investors could see that Bandag had come up with a complete system, which was absolutely unique to the industry and unusual for business in general." The dealer production/sales model allowed for a relatively low capital investment on the part of both Bandag and the dealers themselves.

*"In certain ways, at least from the stock analysts' perspective, at the time of the initial stock offering there simply was no competition. Bandag had roared into free market space."*
*— Warren Heidbreder*

The actual ticker tape retrieved from the NYSE floor as BDG made its debut on Wall Street.

ADMITTED TO THE LIST AND TO DEALINGS BANDAG INCORPORATED COMMON STOCK PAR VALUE TICKER SYMBOL BDG POST SEC F NEW YORK STOCK EXCHANGE INC
$1 10

"In certain ways, at least from the stock analysts' perspective, at the time of the initial stock offering there simply was no competition. Bandag had roared into free market space."

The media dubbed Bandag "the darling of Wall Street" because, in contrast to the hand-to-mouth desperation of the early years, the publicly held company now consistently generated a strong cash flow with virtually no debt.

Sales revenue grew dramatically, mirroring the volume of production.

Bandag was doing everything right. It added new dealers all over the world, then trained and supported them so that they mirrored the Bandag values and vision. At home, Bandag was a powerful force fighting for favorable legislation on issues like excise tax exemption for retreads and tire standards. Abroad, the company

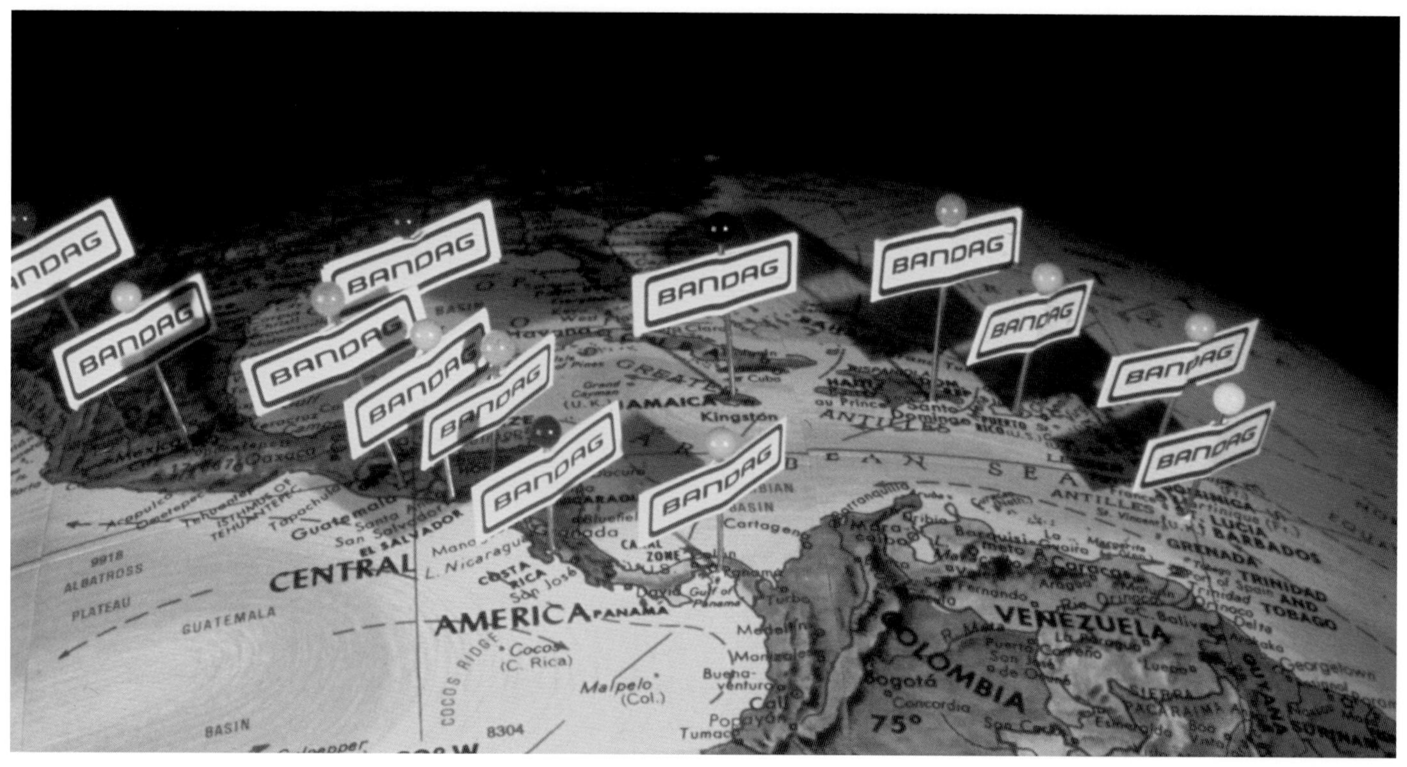


Bandag not only took the US by storm, but also spread quickly around the world.

Roy Carver official opens a new plant i Leon, Mexico as Banda plant representative and communi leaders look o

Vitafrio

*"The Lord helped me be a good salesman. Sometimes I'd be talking to a prospect and I'd pray to myself, and then I could see the conversation shift. Then I'd make the sale."*
*— Harold Vischer*

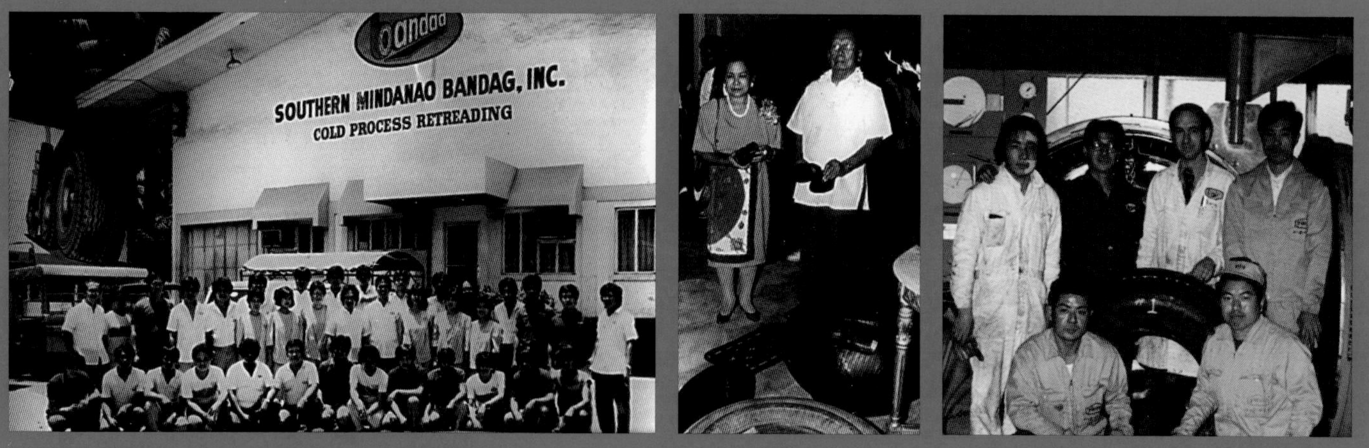


Scores of new dealers were added throughout both Americas, Europe, Africa, Australia and the Far East. Many dealers added production capacity at a record pace. While motor vehicle registration outside the US was also booming, the need for world famous Bandag® retreads continued to grow.

made wise decisions in opening new markets despite language, cultural and political barriers. The end users were always kept in mind, and they appreciated quality products that clearly added to their bottom line. A Bandag® tire became exactly what one of the marketing slogans proclaimed: "The world's most trusted retread." And as Bandag grew, it gained business allies, the benefits of economies of scale, and market share.

Harold Vischer recalls that *Barron's* magazine once described Bandag as "the money machine from Iowa. They said that a Bandag franchise was like a license to print money."

"The reason we were better than everybody else," says long-time Bandag employee Ron Seiler, "is that we had the whole process, and we set down very precise rules for it. We led the industry with specs, rules and standards — we could do that because we provided it all. We gave the dealers manuals and training second to none. And when radial tires came on the scene, our flexible envelope system could accommodate them. We were already way ahead of the game."

Another thing that set Bandag apart from the competition, says Don Schauer, who edited the *Bandagram*, a magazine for dealers, was Bandag's ability as a problem-solver. "If a fleet customer has a problem with a retread, we solve the problem; other guys just suggest the fleet owner buy new tires."

"Of course, none of this just happened," Vischer says.

"We worked very hard. I'd be traveling, sometimes two or three weeks at a time. I was gone over family birthdays, Thanksgiving, whatever. We made personal contact with 95 percent of the dealers. Well, nobody else did that; nobody worked as hard as we did.

"And we trained our salesmen to talk to the truckers, and the truckers would tell their friends. Then we'd collect testimonials from truckers all over the place, and use those in our advertising. We were, you know, selling service and information as well as a product. And we would reward the dealers with trips, and those guys, they'd buy rubber because they enjoyed the trips.

"The Lord helped me be a good salesman. Sometimes I'd be talking to a prospect and I'd pray to myself, and then I could see the conversation shift. Then I'd make the sale."

In 1969, Bandag sales hit $20 million. In 1973, they had skyrocketed to $95 million, and Bandag was listed 909 on Fortune magazine's list of top 1,000 U.S. industrial corporations. The following year Bandag was cited as "Growth Company of the Year" by the National Association of Investment Clubs; the award was based on three key factors — the company had been in business at least 10 years and publicly owned for five; it had sales, pre-tax profits and earnings growth rates of at least 10 percent; and it was out-performing other companies in its industry.

Bandag and Bandag dealers took a break from the 1973 annual dealer meeting to pose for a group shot in sunny Spain.

*"The reason we were better than everybody else is that we had the whole process, and we set down very precise rules for it.... And when radial tires came on the scene, our flexible envelope system could accommodate them. We were already way ahead of the game."*
— Ron Seiler

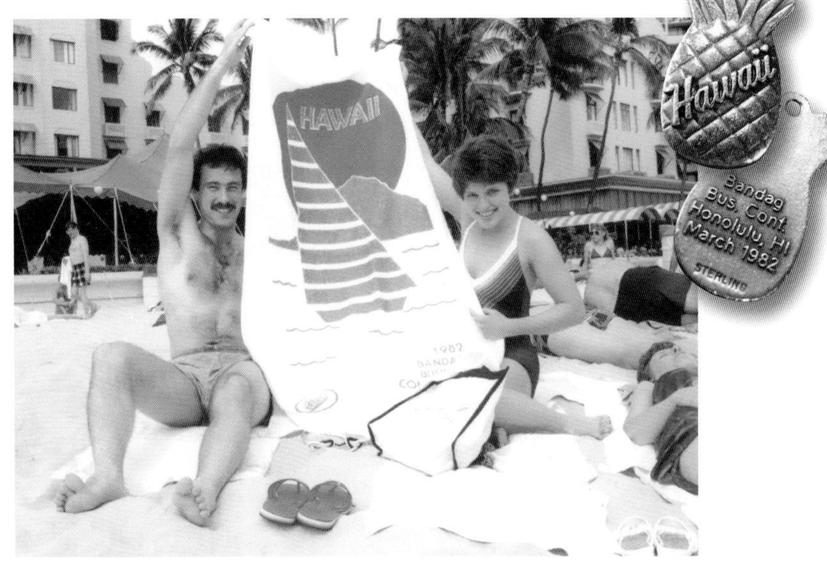


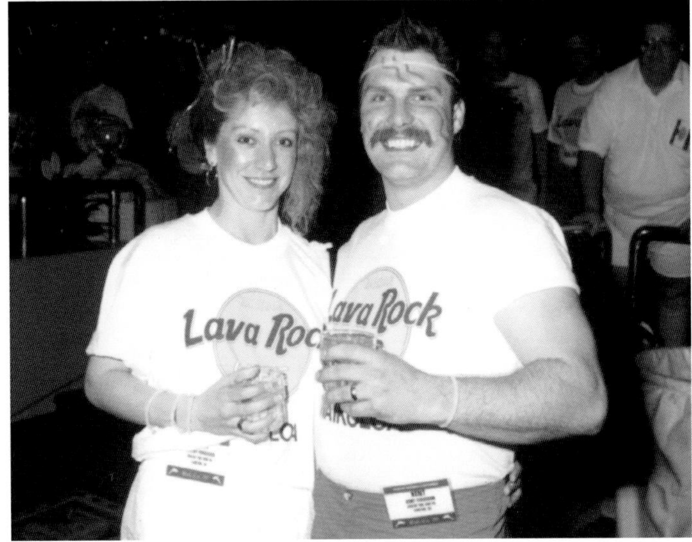


There's a lot to be learned at a dealer conference, but you know what they say about all work and no play....

Pierre Debroux, F
Carver, Bill Kehoe
of Bill Kehoe Tire C
Savannah, Georg
Harold Vischer a
Charlie Edwa
paused for a pict
before dinner at
dealer conferer
in 19

Martin Carver (left) joins the Board of Directors to work on future plans for the fast-growing company.

FORTUNE
THE FORTUNE
500
THE LARGEST U.S. INDUSTRIAL CORPORATIONS



In 1976 sales reached $182 million. A decade later they stood at $370.3 million. In 1991 Bandag was placed on the Fortune 500 list of largest industrial companies in the U.S. In 1996 Bandag sales had reached nearly $757 million, and Tire Distribution Systems, Inc., the newly formed, wholly owned Bandag subsidiary comprising five Bandag-owned dealerships, racked up an additional $366 million. Bandag was a billion dollar baby.

Of course, the investors loved it. Not only did the stock splits and stock price increases pump up the value of their investment, but they also rejoiced that Bandag had steadily paid quarterly dividends since 1976. In fact, 2006 was the 29th year in which Bandag increased its annual dividend rate; in 1976 it was $0.05, and in 2006 it was $0.335 per share or approximately $6.5 million. Bandag was in the top 2.5 percent of U.S. dividend-paying companies and was consistently recognized by analysts as an outstanding dividend achiever.

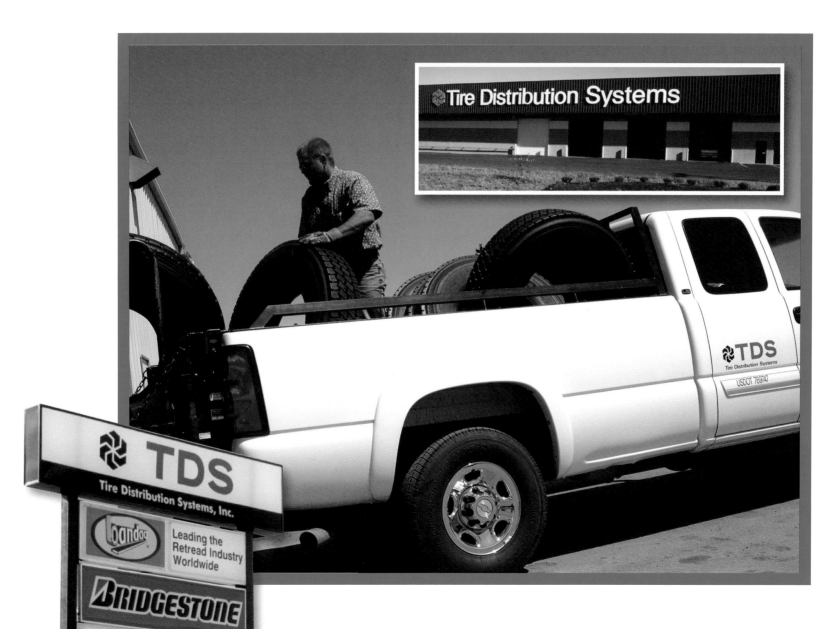


Tire Distribution Systems, Inc. (TDS) was formed as Bandag developed company-owned retread outlets to help fill in areas not covered by franchised dealers.

A single share of Bandag stock purchased in 1968 at $12 became the equivalent of 72 shares which were finally sold for more than $50 a share, over $3,600, not counting what you would have made in dividends. Now, if you'd only bought and held just 1,000 shares in 1968....

You have to wonder how much of that success was envisioned by the board members who attended the first stockholder meeting at the Muscatine Hotel in 1971. They included Roy Carver, Lucille Carver, Eugene Seyb, Harold Vischer, William Cory, Steve Keller and Edgar Jannotta. They were pioneers and risk takers, and they, along with thousands of Bandag employee investors, enjoyed the fruits of their labors. ▪

Generalfeldmarschall (General Field Marshal) Erwin Rommel leads the 15th Panzer Division outside Libya, 1941.

## Following the Desert Fox

When Bandag executives share the "corporate mythology" of their company's origin, they begin with Erwin Rommel, the Desert Fox.

As the story goes, the famed German commander of the Africa Corps during World War II eluded defeat by keeping his vehicles rolling on retreaded tires. That retread process had been invented by a fellow German, Bernard Anton Nowak.

Treads were cured in Germany, then shipped to North Africa where they were bonded to used tire casings — and this is the revolutionary part — with heat no greater than that of the sun-baked desert sands. An army may move on its stomach, but its vehicles move on tires. Field Marshal Rommel, it seems, became a German hero on retreads, and the German military command, we're told, made Nowak a general.

After the war, Nowak established small shops in Germany and further developed his "cold process precured retreading."

While on a business trip to Germany in 1956, Roy Carver met a CIA agent at a wine-tasting party. They decided better wine could be had elsewhere, and getting into a car, Carver spotted the unusual looking tires. He got an earful from the driver about how tough the retreads were, and the next day, "hangover and all," Carver paid a visit to Nowak. Carver soon cut a deal for the American rights to Nowak's process, and four years later obtained the world rights from Nowak's relatives.

From the desert sands of North Africa to the cornfields of Iowa, and the remarkable Bandag story was just beginning. ▪

## Headquarters Designed for Bandag Teamwork

Sure, every company says its most important resource is people, but Bandag has worked diligently from the beginning to give more than lip service to valuing its human resources. Consider the design of Bandag headquarters in Muscatine, Iowa.

When the building was dedicated in 1977, the corporate brochure signed by founder Roy J. Carver and president & CEO Harker Collins gave credit for Bandag's success to its employees.

"The single most important asset of a company, any company, is one that never appears on a balance sheet. It is seldom touted in the annual report. It is often taken for granted. The single most important asset is its people."

The architectural design was based on the concept that many functions of the international corporation had to be integrated for open communication. The openness of the central stairs "suggests the type of unrestrained unity of all three floors of the Headquarters."

Five rectangular bays were offset along a diagonal line, creating "numerous corner offices, highly desirable to employees." The bays were also highly functional, with portable partitions allowing for easy reconfiguration of office and meeting room space. The layout was described as "practical, portable, private and productive."

It is also very egalitarian and unpretentious. For example, chairman Roy Carver had a modest, even tiny office by most corporate standards.

In presenting its headquarters as a monument to employees, the dedication brochure noted in 1977:

The architects and Roy Carver pose with an illustration of Bandag's new corporate headquarters.

"Bandag people, more than two thousand strong around the world, motivated by an inherent, positive corporate philosophy and their own special esprit de corps, have built a company which, in only 20 years, has become more than a leader in its field. It is a model corporation whose growth has been lauded by mentors of the business world and envied throughout the industry." ▪

Employees celebrated the idea of leaving the sauerkraut factory.

The artist's concept of the Bandag campus-like complex, designed to incorporate a new 56,000 sq. ft. three-story Bandag Headquarters and a 104-room hotel. It provides additional meeting space in a park-like setting. The concept is a close match to the finished complex.

Harker Collins, President and CEO addresses the crowd during the ground-breaking ceremony in 1975 at the Bandag World Headquarters site in Muscatine.

Harker and Roy take part in the official groundbreaking.

The skeleton of the corporate headquarters awaits a busy future.

Progress is made quickly on the shell.

Harker and Roy with mayor Evelyn Schauland of Muscatine during the official ribbon cutting ceremony for Bandag's World Headquarters.

The Bandag team is united! Harker Collins and Harold Vischer shown here on the now completed stairway of the Bandag World Headquarters. The openness of the central stairs shows off the type of unrestrained unity of all three floors of the building.

## A DREAM COMPLETED

To commemorate the dedication of the building, which also marked 20 years since its founding, Bandag minted this special coin and distributed it to employees.

1957-197
In its new Wor
Headquarters campu
Bandag completed i
first 20 years, lookin
forward to a new e
but remaining firm
committed to providin
the highest quali
products and service

22
bandag
Jamison Engines
Denny
LONG
Micro Industries
CAMEL
22
GT
Bob Dietz
PAINT STORE

The most remarkable
ıchievement of the
3andag® retreads on
Denny Long's Corvette
vas a six-hour
ndurance race at
Vatkins Glen, NY.
Here a single set of
3andag retreads went
ll the way, carrying
ong to an eighth
lace finish. The
mazing fact was that
nost cars in the field
sed an average of
ree sets of tires
uring the race.
he same set of
etreads took Long
o a 10th-place finish
t a race in Elkhart
ake, Wisconsin a
eek later.

## Racing Boosts Retreads' Reputation

Proudly displayed at the Bandag Learning Center in Muscatine is a well-restored 1968 Corvette sporting the number 22. It's a meaningful piece of Bandag history, recalling the years when Bandag proved the quality of its product through automotive racing.

Soichiro Honda, founder of the Honda Motor empire, liked to say, "Racing improves the breed." Honda credits many of its technological advances to lessons learned on the track, compiling an especially impressive record in Formula One racing. Well, Bandag didn't particularly use race tracks for R&D, though certainly racing confirmed improvements in Bandag processes and products. What racing did for Bandag, though, was improve the reputation of retread tires.

In the mid-'70s Bandag was well on its way to leading the retread truck tire market, but thousands of hot cappers were involved in supplying retreads to passenger vehicles. Although the economics didn't really work to take Bandag into the passenger vehicle market, the company knew it had to battle a common perception that retread tires on cars or trucks were unreliable. The stigma against retreads had remained in the public consciousness ever since the World War II era of rubber rationing, but Bandag was determined to change that notion.

Utilizing a national advertising campaign that included network television, Bandag began to position itself apart from the hot cappers with the message: "Remember the name — Bandag. It will change your ideas about retreads." To imbed that message into public awareness, Bandag pursued several motor sports to demonstrate the performance and durability of its retreads.

Despite a blistering pace at speeds up to 190 mph, the Bandag® retreads on the front of Denny Long's Corvette wore only 1/32 of an inch after 1,000 miles during the 24 Hour Daytona Classic.

The first time Bandag® tires were used on a race car was January 1973 when Bob Seivert and Bill Loughran put the retreads to the test at the Baja 500 off-road race; the spare tire never touched the ground. That same year at the Pike's Peak Hill Climb, Seivert broke a utility-vehicle class record, and six years later Ken Rice and Hal Sealund won their class at the Baja 1000 in a specially prepared Ford Bronco with Bandag® retreads; 220 vehicles began that race, but only 32 finished it.

Bandag got into drag racing as well, putting retreads on the "rocket-powered" Pollution Packer dragster, sporting 5,000 pounds of thrust. In 1974, the Packer ran the same set of Bandag® retreads all season and set a land speed record in Albuquerque, New Mexico, of 322.58 miles per hour in 5.11 seconds in the quarter mile.

Bandag won at truck racing, too. In 1976 Tyrone Malone broke the world land speed record for diesel trucks at a blistering 144 mph in his "Super Boss" Kenworth. In 1988, the "Bandag Bandit," driven by Bandag's chairman, Martin Carver, broke the Super

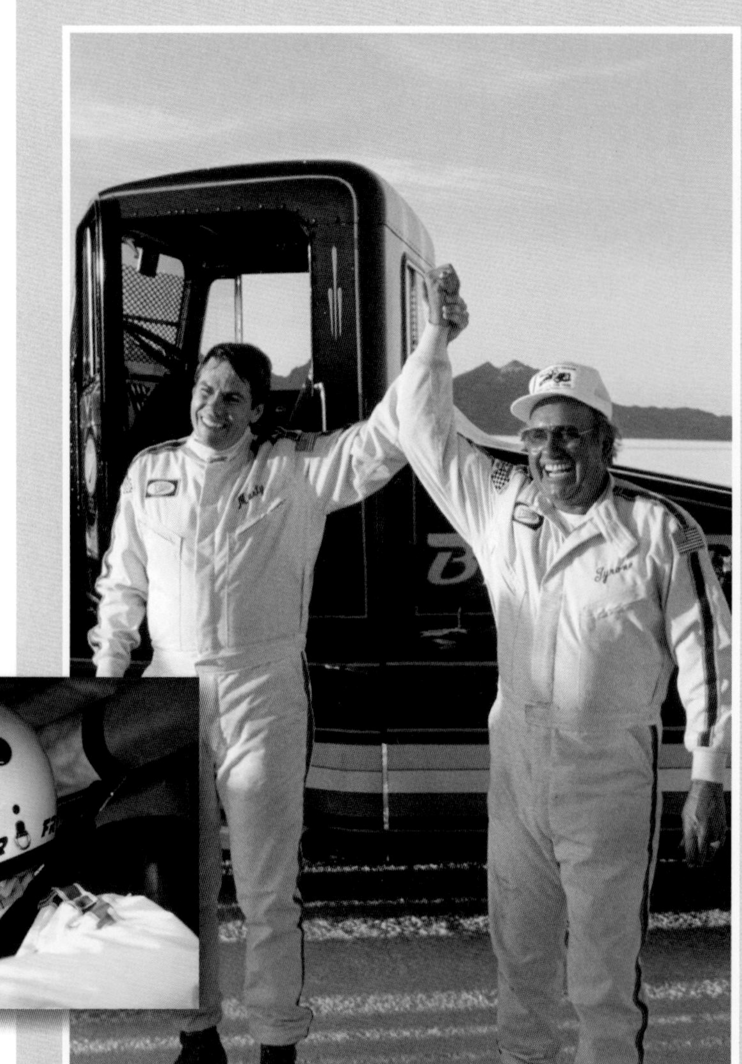

Arms raised in victory, the Bandag Diesel Racing Team celebrated its new world land speed record: 150.918 mph. Driven by Martin Carver, Bandag Chairman, and coached by Tyrone Malone, the Bandit shot down the flats equipped with Bandag® retreads in all wheel positions.

Boss's record at 158.2 mph. Fast forward to 2005, and the Bandag Bullet, from Australia, set a world record for conventionally powered trucks, with an average speed of 182.14 kph over one kilometer from a standing start.

Still, the off-road, dragster and truck races didn't have huge public appeal, so in 1975 Bandag seized another opportunity.

Denny Long, from Sterling, Illinois, one of the top five drivers in Sports Car Club America's 1974 ratings, was racing a 1968 Corvette on road courses across America in the Trans Am Sports Car series, which featured cars everybody was familiar with like Mustangs, Corvettes and Camaros.

Bandag® retreads were tested on Long's Corvette, and soon the Corvette, sporting a fresh Bandag blue and gold paint job, was competing on Bandag Micro-Siped® passenger street retreads. Long's car competed in more than 20 races in two years. The other Trans Am drivers had tires of specially-compounded materials that provided sticking traction but seldom lasted more than 100 miles. In contrast, Bandag® retreads were built to last. In one contest, "24 Hours of Daytona," Long didn't change his Bandag retreads until the 12th hour of the race.

When the Bandag sponsorship ended, the Bandag Corvette eventually was sold to another racer and later became a collector's item. In 2004, when the restored Corvette came up for sale, Bandag jumped to buy it.

The Bandag Corvette is a fine metaphor not only for the quality of Bandag products but also for the company's ability to change public perceptions about retreading and thereby reform an entire industry. Racing helped Bandag earn respect and "improved the breed." ▪

Malone with what was billed as the "Million Dollar Truck Display."

## Tyrone Malone Boosts Dealer Morale

Many Bandag old timers, including longtime dealers, talk about Jerry "Tyrone" Malone, who in 1976 set a world land speed record for diesel trucks at a blistering 144 miles per hour. He did it in his "Super Boss" Kenworth outfitted, of course, with Bandag® retreads. But what they talk about is his extensive promotional tours in North America, Europe and Australia, representing the "Bandag Diesel Racing Team."

George "Bud" Wilkins, who served as manager of the Canadian sales division, was a personal friend of Malone's. "Tyrone did three cross-country tours here, and I think he had more success here than anywhere. We'd get the dealers lined up, they'd invite all the truckers they could, park millions of dollars' worth of fancy trucks around a dealership, and literally hundreds of people would show up. We'd take the truckers on a shop tour and show them the entire Bandag process. The next year our sales would be dramatically higher."

Wilkins says Malone was always the show stopper. "He would cook dinner for everybody, 50 steaks at a time, maybe feed three or four hundred people at an open house. Then he would give a speech, like a carnival huckster, except what he said was true."

Harold Vischer says Malone exemplified the principle that if you want to sell, you have to see people face to face. "But he was a character. The more he drank, the better our retreads got."

What he said about Bandag, though, he could back up. "He'd climb into his 'Super Boss,'" Wilkins says, "rev it up to like 130 miles an hour and do burnouts in the parking lot. He showed everybody Bandag retreads stood up better than new tires."

Malone, a terrific showman, a great promoter and an even better salesman, began his career in the trucking industry in 1969 hauling "Little Irvy," a frozen 38-foot whale. He charged 35 cents to get a close-up view of a real whale.

Malone's appeal was not just with truckers and truck fans. He was a celebrity with people everywhere.

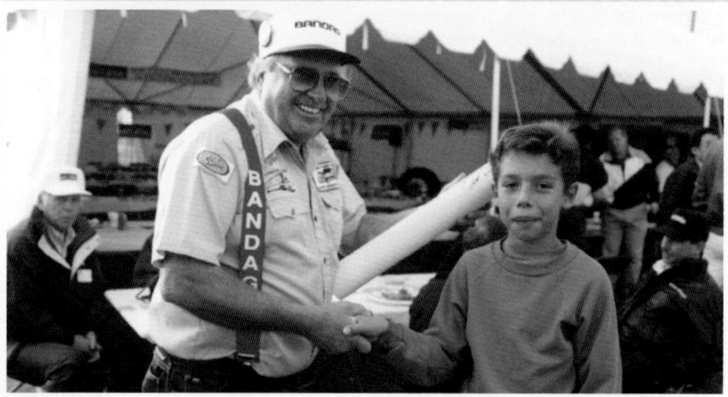


Tyrone Malone's roa show "packed th house." Here at Chicago Bandag ope house, Malon entertained the crow and then climbe into the Super Bo and did burnou in the stree

During one period Malone acquired a huge whale, froze it and took it on tour in a 45-foot refrigerated trailer. "The guy was a showman, that's for sure. The truckers loved him, and that did a lot for Bandag."

Malone continued the Bandag promotional tours for more than a decade. The former used car salesman turned diesel truck race driver died in 1997 when his car collided, ironically, with a truck. ▪

Equipped with Bandag® retreads, Tyrone Malone's Super Boss ran the Bonneville at 144.4 mph to win the World's Fastest Truck title and earn his way into racing fame. Several publications have detailed his accomplishments and career.

Booze
Super Boss
Thermo King

Bandag Bandit
Hobby Kits
Tyrone MaLone
bandag

Bandag Bandit
bandag

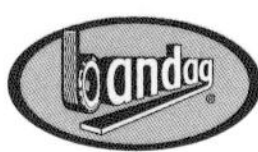

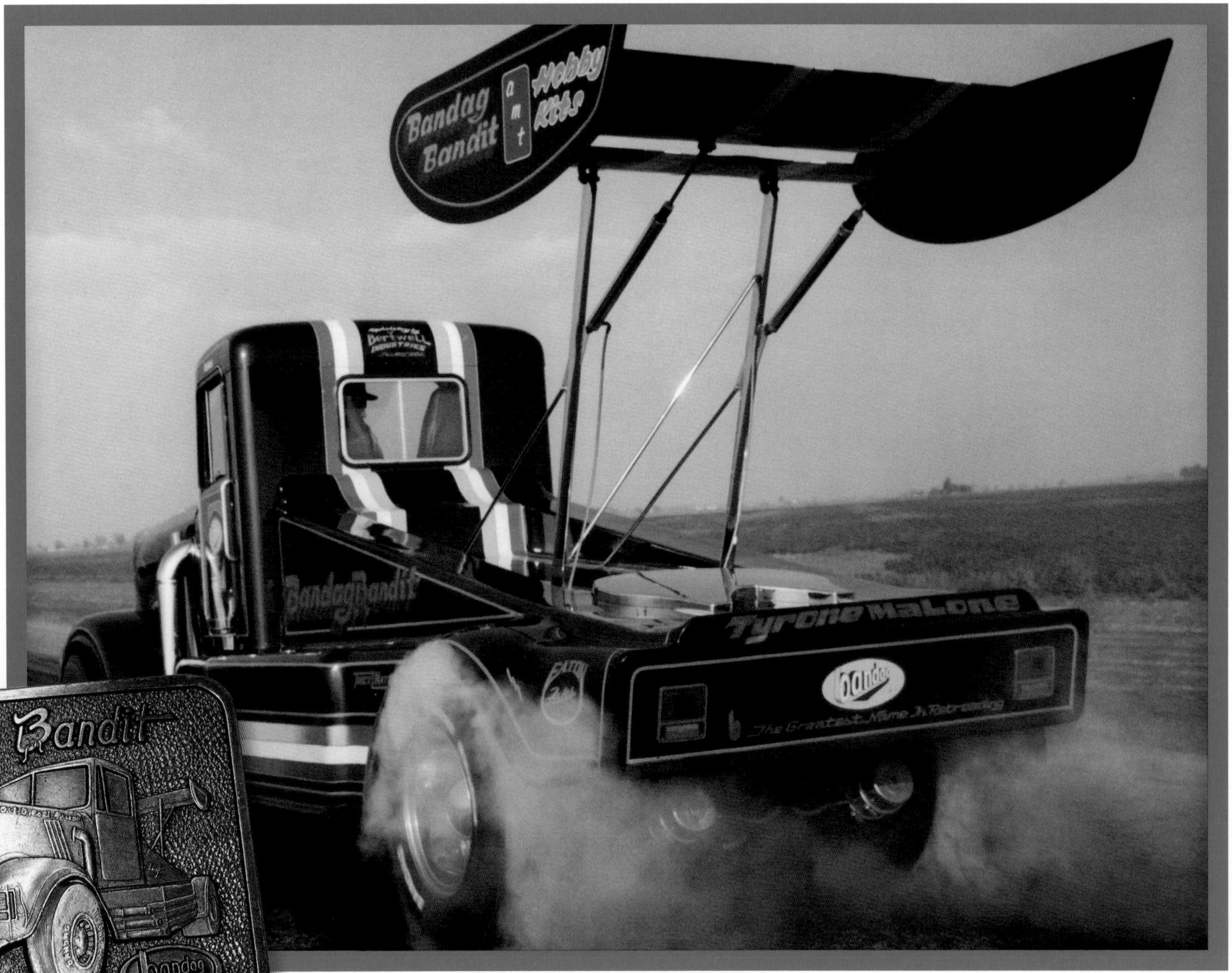

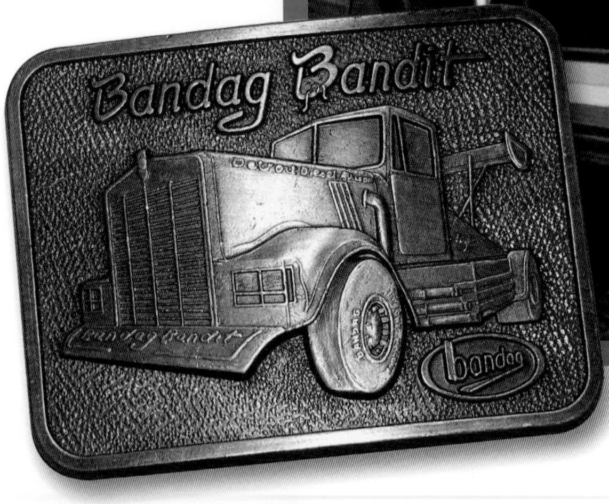

## BANDAG FEELS THE NEED FOR SPEED

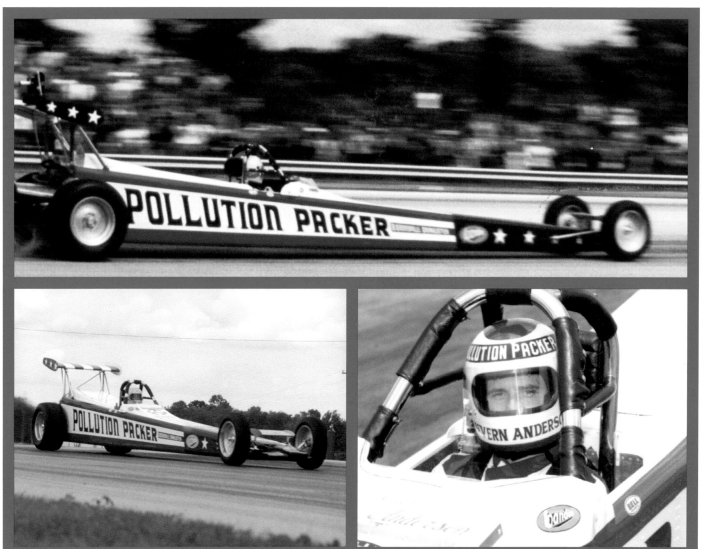

In the summer of 1974, Bandag equipped an 800-pound, 27-foot rocket- powered dragster and attained speeds well over 300 mph in a quarter mile.

The driver, Vern Anderson piloted the Pollution Packer to a top speed of 322.58 mph. During this high-speed run company engineers estimate the bond between casing and tread withstood more than 65,000 pounds of centrifugal force!

In the late '70s Bandag sponsored the Bob Bondurant School of High Performance Driving. The fleet of Datsun "Z" cars and 710 sedans ran exclusively on Bandag® retreads. The Bondurant School, known for its commitment to safety, demanded that only the finest products be used in its cars.

Driver Bob Seivert finished the Baja race on the same four Bandag® retreads with no tire problems. Below, the Bandag Baja Racing Team proudly posed with the race-proven vehicle.

352

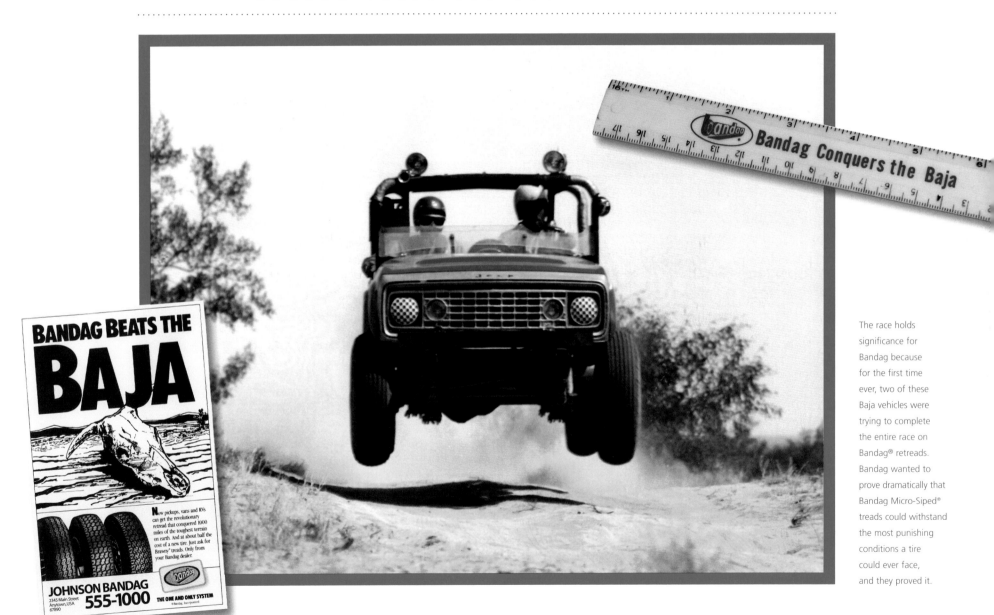

Bandag Conquers the Baja

BANDAG BEATS THE BAJA

Now pickups, vans and RVs can get the revolutionary retread that conquered 1000 miles of the toughest terrain on earth. And at about half the cost of a new tire. Just ask for Brawny® treads. Only from your Bandag dealer.

JOHNSON BANDAG
2345 Main Street
Anytown, USA
67890
555-1000

THE ONE AND ONLY SYSTEM

The race holds significance for Bandag because for the first time ever, two of these Baja vehicles were trying to complete the entire race on Bandag® retreads. Bandag wanted to prove dramatically that Bandag Micro-Siped® treads could withstand the most punishing conditions a tire could ever face, and they proved it.

## BANDAG FEELS THE NEED FOR SPEED

Bandag challenged the Pikes Peak Hill Climb, the Parker 400 and both the Baja 500 and 1000 and came away a winner.

Bandag had built brand awareness first on the road, and then in the sky. Piloted by Muscatine native Tom Oreman, the Bandag Balloon flew across the famed Bermuda Triangle in one promotional feat.

CHAPTER FOUR:

LEADING THE RETREAD INDUSTRY WORLDWIDE

# A BRAND KNOWN AROUND THE WORLD

*Roy Carver developed a global perspective flying overseas during and after World War II, doing business for Carver Pump and Carver Foundry Products. Predictably, soon after he got the Bandag plant running in Muscatine, he looked at the world outside.*

*Within two years he signed up Ambrosiani Brothers, San Juan, Puerto Rico, as the first franchised dealership outside the U.S., then A.B. Stockholm, Stockholm, Sweden, as the first one in Europe. By 1968 Bandag had franchised dealers in 25 countries. Also within that first decade, manufacturing operations, as well as dealerships, were set up outside the U.S. Bandag's first company-owned tread rubber plant apart from Muscatine, began operating in Shawinigan, Quebec, in 1967.*

Carver himself made many of the early contacts in other countries and cemented those relationships with his personal friendship. For one thing, he had taught himself to speak several languages, but his fascination with people and big-hearted concern for their well-being was also a real driving factor. He was able to move comfortably among the locals, without pretense, and people of other cultures took to him. He would stay in the homes of dealers in Latin America, calling their children by name and helping them out in various ways. People in the streets would cheer when Roy Carver came to town.

Roy built the international business segment by cultivating personal relationships, even learning several languages.

orldwide, more
ight moved on
ndag® retreads
an on any other
tread brand.

Tita Coffman, who supported international operations for Bandag, especially in Latin America, says many of the early dealers "had a strong love for Bandag because they had been cultivated by Roy Carver himself. Carver's humanity was very evident; he would joke with them, have coffee in their homes. Those dealers just loved him." For years afterward, Tita Coffman says, market surveys in those countries revealed that the Bandag brand represented quality and reliability. "That started with the efforts of Roy Carver and was sustained by a lot of Bandag people after him."

Setting up manufacturing operations, let alone bringing to point an entire system of production, sales and distribution outside the U.S. is hardly an easy deal. It requires getting to understand the market, economic factors, tariffs and taxes, available resources and how to tap them, figuring out financial opportunities and constraints, and, without question, making allies politically. Tariffs, for example, delayed full development of Bandag in Australia despite an eagerness for a Bandag presence among the Australians as early as 1962. Success in countries outside the U.S. is also largely a matter of what Bill Block, director of corporate communications, calls "orchestrating the culture."

In 1967, this plant in Shawinigan, Quebec became the first location outside the U.S. to produce tread rubber.

Bandag sales literature was printed in many languages to keep pace with the growing number of foreign markets.

Martin Carver, holding true to Bandag culture, attended many grand openings like this one at the Sao Paulo, Brazil rubber plant in 1988.

"In some ways getting established is more about doing the market research than it is about sales ability," Tita Coffman adds. "There's just so much you need to know before you can start to roll."

Patricio Andrade-Marin, who was called out of retirement in 1989 to establish Bandag in Brazil after other efforts there failed, says that keys to success abroad are flexibility and a long-term view. This is not always easy when, as a public company, you are at the mercy of shareholders and hence short-term decisions.

"You have to be extremely careful not to apply short term results but to be strategic," says Andrade-Marin, who later was in charge of Bandag operations for all Latin America. "One of the first things is to determine the real size of the market. Most managers understate the size in order to look good. But I don't believe in those untruths.

## Global Company — Global Manufacturing

As Bandag spread its network of franchised dealers beyond America's borders, it was only a matter of time before demand for Bandag tread rubber and equipment — and the significant import duties Bandag was paying to supply dealers in foreign countries — justified additional manufacturing capacity outside the U.S.

The first international manufacturing facility was a tread rubber plant built in Shawinigan, Quebec, Canada in 1967. In 1971, another plant was built, this time in Lanklaar, Belgium. Additional facilities appeared in South Africa, Australia, New Zealand, Brazil, Mexico, Venezuela, Malaysia, Indonesia, not to mention joint ventures started in a number of other countries. The Bandag brand was expanding rapidly around the globe.

Bandag manufacturing facilities attracted significant attention from the regions and countries where they were built. Vincente Fox, then governor of Leon, Mexico (and later president of Mexico) was on hand for the grand opening of Bandag's tread manufacturing operation, Vitafrio, in 1982. The company clearly had gained a worldwide reputation for success and communities showed their appreciation for Bandag's contributions to their local economies.

Ironically, while Bandag's success was largely due to the standardization of a retreading process the world over, their manufacturing techniques around the world were hardly standardized at all. In fact, some plants purposely took very independent steps to meet unique needs of the customers and markets they served, with little or no regard for the impact these decisions would have on Bandag's manufacturing system costs.

Nate Derby, Senior Vice President, Manufacturing-Design until he retired from Bandag in 2004, had joined the company as an engineer. He eventually found himself in charge of all of Bandag's manufacturing facilities worldwide.

Nate Derby (right) is presented a "Presidents Club" plaque by Maurice McGuire, Vice President of Manufacturing.

Through the eyes of an engineer, Nate saw that Bandag's manufacturing processes were capable of tremendous productivity, but the inconsistent methods, multiple raw material suppliers and one-off tread rubber formulations were hampering efficiency and limiting cost controls. Two major changes would help the company become more competitive and efficient:

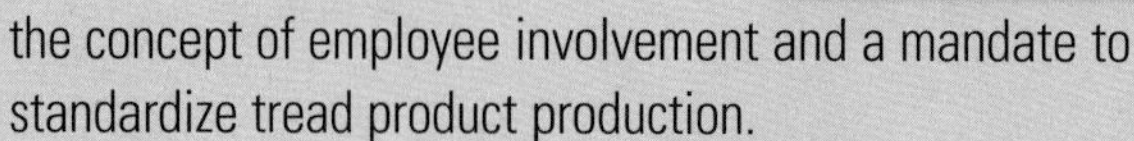

the concept of employee involvement and a mandate to standardize tread product production.

"The initiative to involve plant employees in problem-solving teams had very positive effects at the plants because the workers had real ownership in the improvements," said Nate. "That sort of teaming has become the standard practice now, and it's a real asset to Bandag."

Nate Derby had an even more direct effect on Bandag's success with one simple instruction to the global tread manufacturing team: standardization is not an option. As the industry evolved, the combination of higher plant productivity plus escalating raw material and energy prices made the economics of standardization all the more brilliant.

Eventually business conditions plus improved plant productivity forced Bandag to make difficult decisions, such as closing plants in Muscatine, Iowa, Shawinigan Quebec and Chino, California. But Bandag's excellence in manufacturing helped the company to hold competitors at bay by delivering top quality products and customer satisfaction day after day the world over. ▪

## THE PRESIDENT'S CLUB

Bandag held Plant Manager meetings to share ideas, discuss production issues and recognize outstanding performance.

BANDAG INCORPORATED WORLD HEADQUARTERS

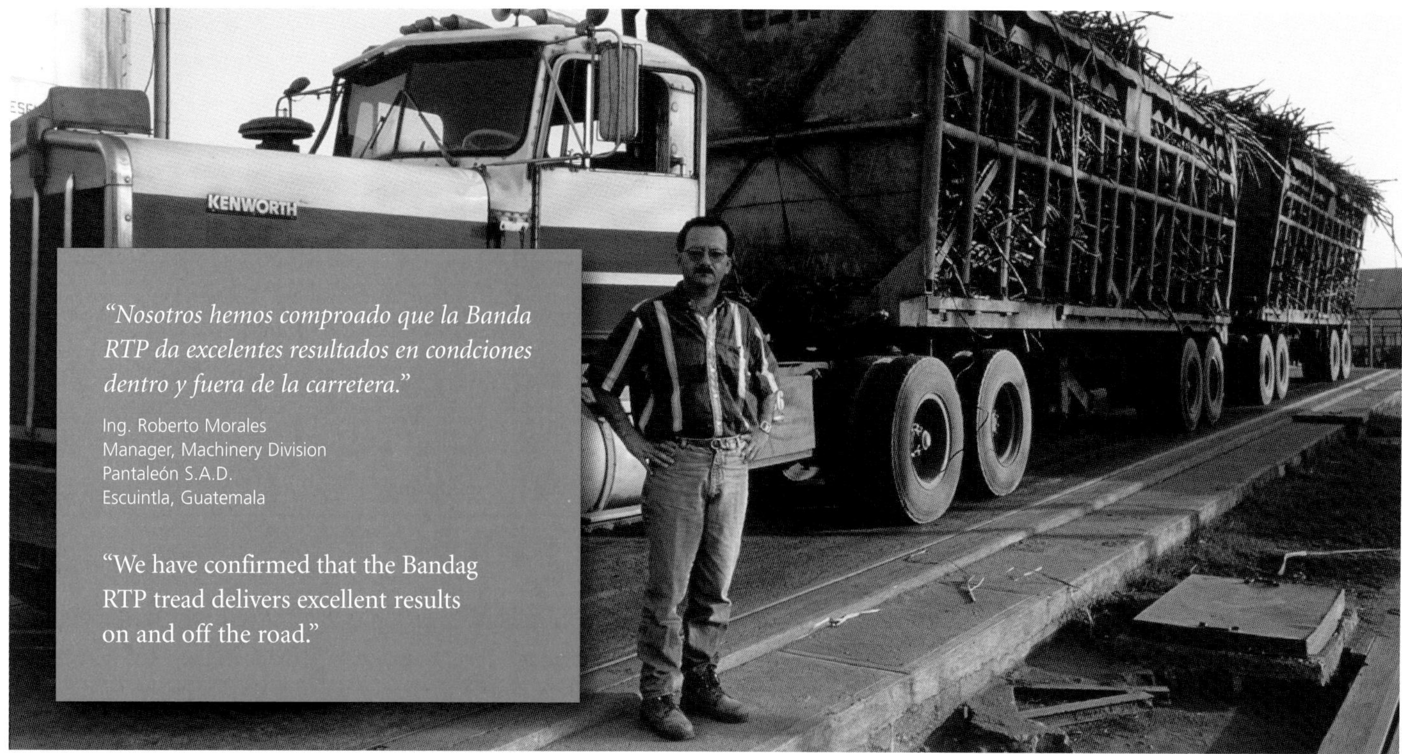

KENWORTH
"Nosotros hemos comproado que la Banda RTP da excelentes resultados en condciones dentro y fuera de la carretera."
Ing. Roberto Morales
Manager, Machinery Division
Pantaleón S.A.D.
Escuintla, Guatemala
"We have confirmed that the Bandag RTP tread delivers excellent results on and off the road."


Taken from the 1994 Bandag Annual Report, this testimonial bears witness to the quality and flexibility of Bandag tread products.

So in Brazil, for example, we set ourselves what seemed an impossible goal. And then we went ahead and attained it, going from 2 percent to 20 percent market share in about three years." How did he do it? One of the first things was to "clean up" the business ethics. Andrade-Marin says that in many countries exchanging money under the table is the accepted way of doing business. "Most companies charge a big number up front for the franchise and then a royalty. Bandag doesn't do that. I had to make sure that our employees wouldn't explain to the dealer there was no upfront fee, and they would line their pockets with money or cars or trips, and the dealer just thought that was normal." That was not the Bandag way, so Andrade-Marin fired the entire sales staff when he took over in Brazil.

Next he determined the nature of his market and

highlight for many of ndag's international alers and managers :luded a visit to the uscatine World adquarters.

*"You have to keep an open line to the government, and you have to keep communicating that you are doing something good for the country. You highlight the benefits of sharing your technology, the benefits to transportation, to business, to employment, and you contribute to their communities in various ways."*
*— Pat Andrade-Marin*

TrenTyre operated Bandag's largest chain of dealerships in South Africa.

its economies. "You have to understand that most of the world, at least in the early '90s, was cash poor and labor rich, while the U.S. was just the opposite. We went after successful people we didn't have to finance because inflation in Brazil was so high." Bandag dealers in Brazil increased from 12 dealers to 175, none of them financed by Bandag. Andrade-Marin adds that in Latin America the target was successful families, people who had cash and wanted to invest it, not to please stockholders, but for the sake of their children and grandchildren.

Still another key was cultivating good relationships throughout the country, even with competitors. "Competition is an American cultural phenomenon, but the rest of the world isn't necessarily like that." For example, one time when the government banned the importing of rubber to support local sources, Andrade-Marin got a friend to call a new tire company, and Bandag had a supply of rubber within 48 hours. "To be successful in foreign markets you have to be flexible and creative."

Having good relations with governments is also extremely important. "Because governments are centralized, they listen to complaints from the various sides and take a side," Andrade-Marin says. "You have to keep an open line to the government, and you have to keep communicating that you

"Never stop running." The old Chinese proverb implied that if you stop or slow down, you will get behind.

Martin Carver (left) and executives from Bandag de Mexico attend the grand opening of a Bandag retread facility in Mexico.

*"In every case Bandag became a brand name known for delivering extraordinary value."*
*— Frederico Kopittke*

are doing something good for the country. You highlight the benefits of sharing your technology, the benefits to transportation, to business, to employment, and you contribute to their communities in various ways. Using that approach we were able to leverage [such good will] into getting what we needed" in much of Latin America.

Frederico Kopittke, Bandag's vice president, International, agrees that understanding the lay of the land culturally and politically is critical. "There is a delicate balance between serving the fleet, supporting the needs of dealers, and coping with realities of volatile economies," says Kopittke. "In South Africa, where our first dealer opened in 1962, Bandag has seen tremendous political economic change. In Brazil, we have witnessed inflation as high as 35% per month. Yet in every case Bandag became a brand name known for delivering extraordinary value."

“You’d see a vehicle with a Bandag sticker downtown in an Asian city. We were recognized everywhere.”
– Hoz Vischer

The Bandag brand enjoyed international recognition as evidenced by this city bus in Costa Rica.

Working at the level of the people meant acceptance, cooperation and growth. By 1978 Bandag had 859 dealerships and franchises in 51 countries, and a decade later the figure stood at 1,043 franchised dealer shops in 103 countries. As the 21st century neared Bandag had its own manufacturing facilities in Australia, Belgium, Brazil, Canada, India, Indonesia, Malaysia, Mexico, Venezuela, Sri Lanka and South Africa, as well as plants in six locations in the U.S.

“Hoz” Vischer, Harold’s son, who was involved in Bandag advertising for several years, says that the Bandag brand is recognized in remote corners of the globe. “You’d see a vehicle with a Bandag sticker downtown in an Asian city, or on a kid’s bicycle. We were recognized everywhere.”

Bandag is a worldwide brand. ▪

Bandag plants worldwide, such as the Lanklaar facility in Belgium, showed their pride in the brand by proudly incorporating it into their building design.

## Bandag in Europe — Managing Complexity

Bandag's steady growth in Europe testifies to the company's ability to drive across an incredibly diverse economic, monetary, cultural, lingual, regulatory and political landscape. What's more, the rules of the road were constantly changing.

Beginning in the 1960s, Bandag was franchising in Germany, the United Kingdom and Scandinavia, "with salesmen all over the place." Later the company established dealerships in Italy, Spain and France, and — with the collapse of the Soviet Bloc — countries of Eastern Europe, including the Czech Republic, Romania and Russia. Countries in northern Africa and the Middle East, which had strong economic ties with European countries, also were part of the picture.

Bandag executives like Jim Lemkau, who went to Europe from Muscatine in 1987, and Gary Carlson, who served in Europe in the mid-1990s, recall the way things evolved for Bandag over the decades; the advent of the European Union and the fall of the Iron Curtain were two of the most significant developments.

The first thing Bandag personnel had to learn was that Europeans, by and large, conduct business more conservatively than do

The Bandag process ensured a uniform look and quality wherever Bandag® retreads were produced.

Belgian dealer Visé Pneu celebrated its 45th Anniversary as a dealer. Pictured are Françis Letawe & André Gehlen.

Americans. High taxation and tight regulations in Europe, along with the complexities of many national identities, are factors that slow down business transactions. Lemkau illustrates the difference:

"If I'm selling a product in the U.S., I talk about its great features and the benefits to the client's revenue stream and all that, and the American pulls his wallet out of his pocket, plops it on the table and says, 'Wow, it looks like I could make a lot of money with this opportunity.' In contrast, the European listens and questions and listens and questions and sits on his wallet and says, 'Oh my, I could sure lose a lot of money with all this risk.' Europeans need much more assurance, you have to keep backing them up along the way, and trust is a very big issue."

Carlson addresses the complexity this way: "Bandag was full-fledged in Europe by the 1960s, and of course with Europe's huge potential we had to work the market no matter what the complexity. But that meant, among other considerations, that we needed to have staff trained in 24 or 25 languages; in fact, practically everyone in our service department had to speak four or five languages. In Belgium, a country one-fifth the size of Iowa, they speak three languages."

High European demand for Bandag products resulted in the addition of numerous distribution markets.

Mike Tirona, Bandag's Europe, Middle East & Africa (EMEA) vice president, notes that the language differences pose plenty of practical and expensive challenges. "With the multitude of languages, every time we renew our laptop computers for the field folks we have to request 20 different keyboards to accommodate the language differences. This is an example of 'our reality,' and managing these differences requires strong focus and discipline."

"And the language issue was complicated not only by the number of languages but also because of cultural understanding of the languages," says Lemkau. "For example, the word 'must' is a very aggressive word in German; you had to be careful in using it so as not to offend people. You had to be a history student to know where people were coming from and what their sensitivities were."

Cultural differences were a challenge. Negotiating a deal required one style in dealing with the Spanish and French, who are stereotypically more emotional, and another style altogether with the solemn Germans. Some countries found the exclusivity requirements acceptable, and others saw them as violations of their freedom. "With our franchises we also found that different countries read them and followed them in different ways,"

This facility in Belgium took full advantage of the powerful Bandag brand.

Carlson remembers. "We would find in one country dealers paid attention to the details and honored their contracts, and in another they would readily sign agreements, but the commitment to them didn't always follow."

"When you sell to Swedes," Lemkau recalls, "you have to talk to everybody in the company; they won't act until everybody down to the janitor says 'we agree.' Farther south in Europe, where there is a much more paternalistic viewpoint, they'll make a decision without telling anybody. The techniques that work well one place fall flat in another."

Of course, when the Iron Curtain came down, doing business in sophisticated West Germany was very different from East Germany where there was little infrastructure. "One of our challenges," Carlson recalls, "was that in the eastern bloc you couldn't figure out who owned property because it had all been controlled by the state. You really had to be adaptable."

Then there was the challenge of different currencies. "Up until the advent of the European Union in 1992 and the 'euro,' every country had its own currency," Lemkau says. "You had to do business with the local money and be constantly watchful of

devaluation, which, obviously, would wreak havoc to the balance sheet. We were constantly figuring out how to hedge against all the currency fluctuations. That, of course, isn't something you worry about in the United States."

Complexities in the trucking industry itself were enormous. Keith Adams, who was general manager for GE's trailer division of 30,000 trailers and the Bandag contact person for the GE tire management contract held from 2002 to 2005, highlights the problem. "The difference for GE in complexity between the U.S. trailer division and the Europe trailer division was that in the U.S. they dealt with approximately five-plus trailer configurations while in Europe they had to manage over 120-plus trailer configurations — and this doesn't even take into account the multitude of different tire sizes."

There was no end to the complexity. Even managing calendars was a challenge. "We had to wrestle with a matrix of 48 national holidays as well as smaller ones," Lemkau remembers. "In Italy, Christmas gift giving is in January, not December, so we never went anywhere to speak of during several weeks in the winter. In many of the countries, people take four to seven weeks vacation. Just working your calendar to make appointments was a full-time job."

Although the advent of the European Union presented an entirely new set of rules — previous agreements formed in the various countries weren't all compliant — the EU helped Bandag pursue a successful competitive strategy. Of course, there were a lot of small retreaders throughout Europe and tough competition from big players like Michelin. Bandag saw that its future hinged on its ability to deliver on the service and equipment side.

"We asked ourselves what we could bring to the party," Lemkau says. "Our franchise relationships were an advantage, but we saw that we really had the upper hand on the technical services side. So we bolstered this, upgrading our gene pool with guys who could fix anything. We also started sourcing equipment in Europe, where automation was in greater demand than in the U.S. In Europe the cost of labor is two to three times what it is in the U.S., so as we emphasized computerization, which had a strong appeal to potential dealers.

"We also emphasized our ability to supply spare parts to avoid production down-time. We would guarantee that we would have the parts and the technicians in shop to install them within two days anywhere from Europe to Kenya to Saudi Arabia. The competition made the dealers wait a week or two for replacement parts. Whether it was new setup or replacement, I believe we always delivered better than the competition. I think that was a huge reason for Bandag's success."

Gaining market share in Europe, Africa, Asia and the Middle East will continue to be a dogfight. Bridgestone's acquisition and on-going support of Bandag will bring greater resources to the fray. ▪

European dealers leveraged their ability to deliver products and services in ways the competition could not match.

F-450
bandag

Bandag's mission statement said it all: "We keep trucks rolling by creating and delivering the best products, services and solutions for our customers."

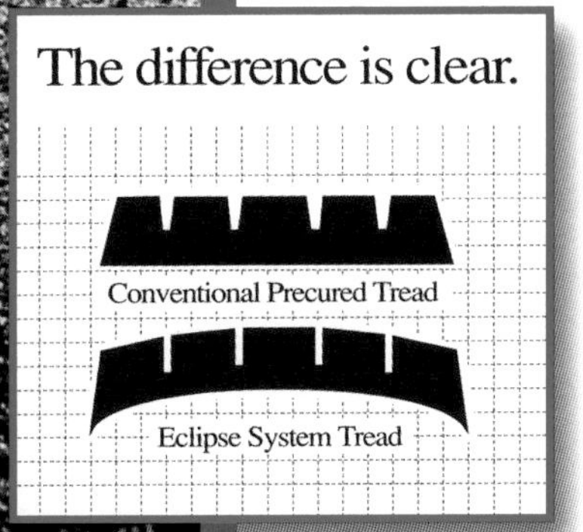

The launch of Bandag's exclusive Eclipse System in 1991 (renamed ECL in 2007) produced a retreaded tire that looked and performed more like a new tire.

bandag

# THE BANDAG STRATEGIC ALLIANCE

*Bandag's greatest strength has always been its independent dealers, but keeping them happy hasn't always been easy, partly because they are, well, independent. So from the earliest days, Bandag concentrated not only on opening new dealerships but on supporting them.*

*"The quality of a leader is reflected in the standards they set for themselves," said Ray Kroc, who knew a thing or two about franchising. If dealers were to become and remain loyal allies, they would have to see rigorous standards consistently applied by the parent company as well as more-than-adequate training and full support in problem solving. As with McDonald's, where the French fries are always hot and salty, for Bandag it was all about consistent customer service, whether you're talking about the immediate customer, the dealer, or the end user, the trucker.*

yle Hayes (l)
Doyle Hayes Tire
vice, poses with
son and daughter
their shop in
ton, Georgia.
yle Hayes became
andag dealer
1968.

Twyla Hartman, franchise services specialist, says: "Our dealers are loyal because they trust us; they know we'll do what it takes to serve them. It may be something as simple as packaging materials the right way, making sure they're well labeled. Our message is, 'We'll walk you through whatever it is.'"

Bill Block, director of corporate communications, says Martin Carver "left a legacy of a collaborative organization that can genuinely serve customers, where employee hearts and minds are driven by customer needs."

Martin Carver addresses the dealer body at an annual Business Conference.

What's more, Block says, "Marty was an icon to many of these dealers. They saw him as one of them. They considered him an independent businessman like themselves. Now Saul Solomon has begun to pick up where Marty's left off, and lead the company."

One thing's for sure. The annual dealer business conference is always a very big deal for the corporate office. Everybody works for months ahead of time to make things go right so that the dealers leave with a good taste in their mouths.

At the first such conference in Honolulu, Gene Seyb, then senior vice president-finance, said that financial analysts recommended Bandag stock because of the strength of the dealer network. "Our management has repeatedly said we have more than a supplier relationship with our dealers. We are in fact partners. There is a counterpart to our dealer partners…our shareholder partners. Bandag management strives to maintain a balance that best serves the objectives of all our partners. But, if we need to lean one way or another, it will always be to the side of our dealers."

And the dealers historically have appreciated all the ways that Bandag helped them become very successful in the tire business.

Bandag used the Dealer Business Conference to launch new products or technology. In 1985 the new OTS computer was intended to help Commercial Salesmen collect data about their customers. At right: the ARC System made its debut, offering real savings to Bandag dealers as it could eliminate the need for rims, flanges or tubes during curing.

John Snider, who now operates nine Bandag dealerships in six states, says he originally wanted to associate with the Muscatine retreader because "it had the right footprint, and you always want to align yourself with the market leader." And he has been pleased with the partnership. "We see Bandag as more than a supplier. It's really an extension of our own business."

Snider sees several aspects to the strong relationship dealers have with Bandag. For one thing, Bandag consistency is a very important factor for him, consistency of product, consistency of service and consistency of leadership.

"Consistency of leadership is something we don't see on the new tire side, but the fact Marty Carver was at the helm so long means we all knew him, we knew what he stood for, and we respect the company because of that. Our industry has changed significantly in the last seven or eight years — with increased competition, new alliances and other changes. Marty provided continuity amid all this change because he delivered a consistent message, and that gave us confidence."

However, the market changes Snider alluded to tested Bandag's relationship with its dealers. An internal

*"We see Bandag as more than a supplier. It's really an extension of our own business."*
*— John Snider*

Long-time Bandag dealer Snider Tire of Greensboro, North Carolina, offers a wide variety of tread products and services to their fleet customers.

*"This company has always been about meeting challenges through innovation. Now we just have to figure out how to provide a wider range of services in a fully coordinated fashion — everything the trucking industry needs."*

— *Martin Carver*

Martin Carver always spoke from the heart, honestly and truthfully, whether the news was good or bad.

document published in 1995, updated in 1996, was called *The Case for Change*. It highlighted the upheaval in the external environment and called upon Bandag to change with the times.

*The Case for Change* noted that globalization meant consumers in both developed and emerging economies demand more for less. Lead times shrink, and costs must be slashed. "Manufacturers turn to their suppliers, including trucking companies, to help them improve their competitive positions," the booklet said. "They put intense pressure on fleets, who must respond to maintain their own competitive positions. They, in turn, demand more from their suppliers, including Bandag and Bandag dealers."

Deregulation of the U.S. trucking industry in 1980, which introduced free market competition to truckers, also had an enormous impact on Bandag. Following a series of legislative acts and court decisions during the '80s, more than 3,000 individuals and companies had jumped into the trucking business by the mid-'90s. Existing fleets expanded terminals and equipment quickly. "Such expansion created overcapacity, depressed shipping rates, and forced 48,000 carriers — including 74 of 1980s top 100 carriers — out of business."

This coin was presented to Bandag employees after the successful completion of an internal training initiative called Acting as Owners.

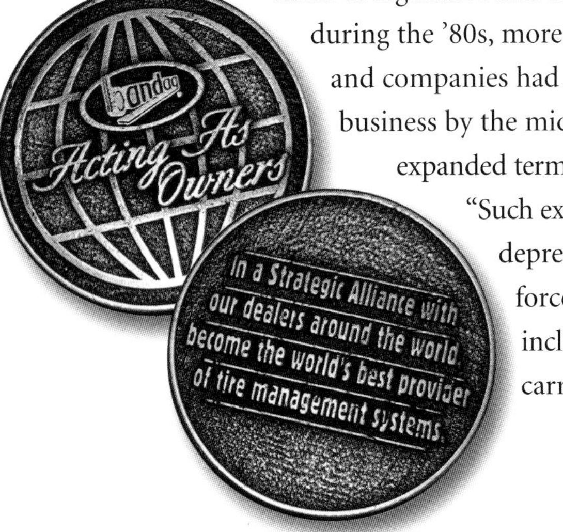


Two other factors were highlighted in the call to action. The increase in intermodal transportation meant that fleets were transporting worldwide via truck, rail, ship and plane with tighter schedules and precise operating requirements. In response, the fleets were driving costs down. "Fleets are unwilling to accept product variation, poor quality, or enroute tire failures. They can't afford problems or hassles. Not in this fiercely competitive environment."

The other pressure highlighted was the growth of leasing, facilitated by changes in tax laws. Because leasing contracts make the leasing company responsible for vehicle maintenance (including tires), a whole new type of Bandag customer emerged — the leasing company.

These changes amounted to a multi-pronged assault on the Bandag dealer network. With the majority of vehicles controlled by giant trucking companies and lease company fleets, purchasing decisions were shifted from the local level, where Bandag dealers operated, to the regional and national level. Unwilling to tolerate the hassle of uneven purchasing contracts, or pricing and delivery from several dealers, the majority of the market, controlled by the big fleets, demanded a direct relationship with Bandag instead of relying on the local dealers.

*"[Manufacturers] put intense pressure on fleets, who must respond to maintain their own competitive positions. They, in turn, demand more from their suppliers, including Bandag and Bandag dealers."*
*— The Case for Change*

Alex Brewer (2nd from right) stands with his sons at Brewer Tire in Colorado.

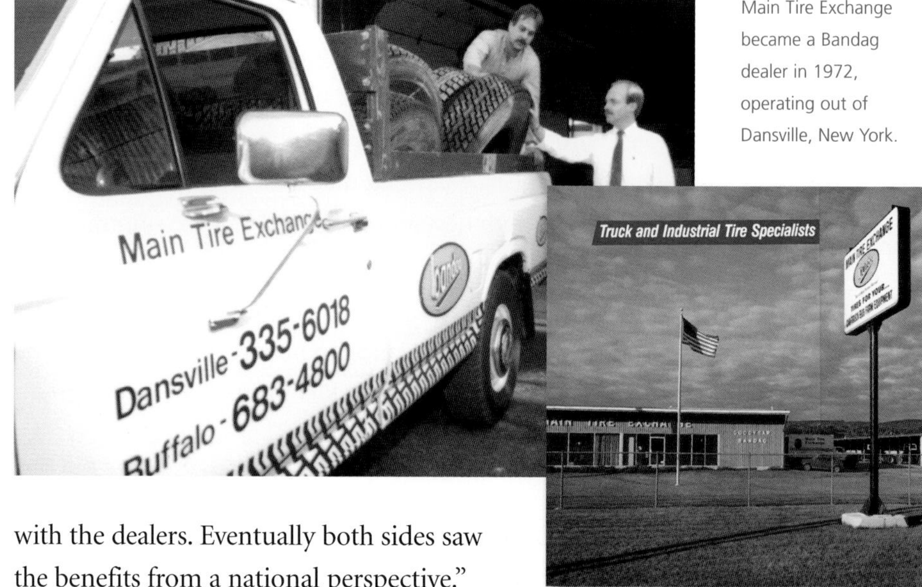


Main Tire Exchange became a Bandag dealer in 1972, operating out of Dansville, New York.

Paul Roots, a widely experienced executive who contributed to *The Case for Change*, says: "A big fleet, like Ryder trucks, had to deal with something like 180 dealers across the country. There was no way they would achieve a standardized program with price, quantity, delivery, warranties, standardized tread designs and the rest. So we wrote a program, got the dealers' permission, and took it to Ryder. That's how we negotiated on behalf of the dealers with the big fleets."

Ike Luna, who worked out the deal from the Ryder end, said: "We got push-back from both Bandag dealers and Ryder because Ryder would have to switch dealers. To make it happen, Martin Carver loaned the company plane so that we could go coast to coast to meet with the dealers. Eventually both sides saw the benefits from a national perspective."

Still, you can begin to see why, in that environment, the corporate relationship with dealers would get more than a little strained. And you can understand that Bandag would have to work as never before to fulfill its marketing slogan "Always Out Front."

One development not anticipated in *The Case for Change* was the direct threat to Bandag when an investment banker attempted to purchase several dealerships, evidently with a view to reselling them. To defend itself, Bandag ended up buying the dealerships then eager to sell to somebody at a premium, and merged them to create the subsidiary Tire Distribution Systems, Inc. (TDS).

Commercial Tire of Boise, Idaho began their Bandag dealership in 1978.

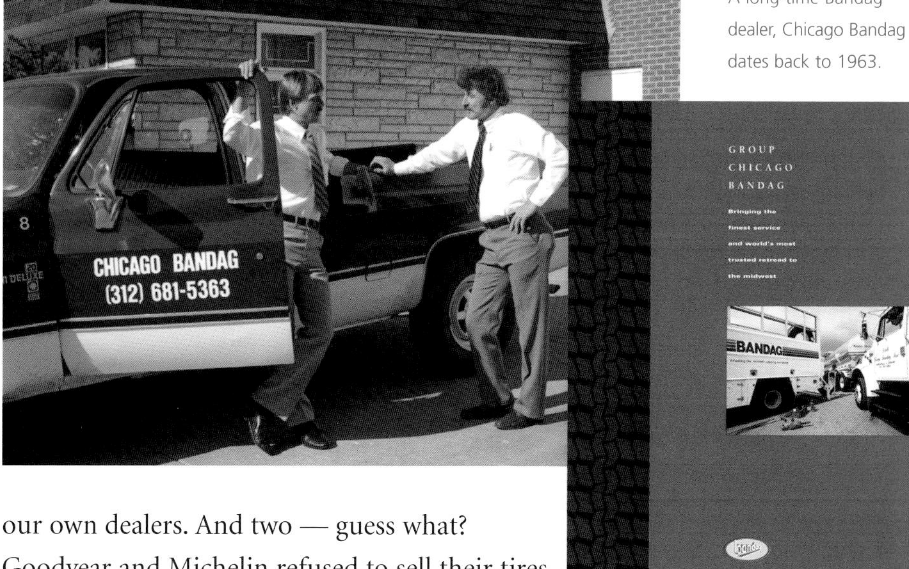


A long-time Bandag dealer, Chicago Bandag dates back to 1963.

This was hardly the first time the competition had tried to buy out Bandag dealers. George "Bud" Wilkins in Canada recalls that Goodyear "took a run at Bandag in the mid-'80s and purchased eight to 10 dealerships. We had to replace them right away to keep them from eating our lunch."

The challenge of owning and operating commercial tire dealerships was formidable. As Warren Heidbreder, Bandag's former chief financial officer, says: "We ended up buying out the dealers, borrowing $100 million to do it. The problem was not only the hit to our financial resources but also the damage to our business model. We had to buy dealerships, which also handled new tires. That meant two things: One, we were now directly competing against our own dealers. And two — guess what? Goodyear and Michelin refused to sell their tires to Bandag-owned TDS," (though, fortunately, Bridgestone chose to support the fledgling company). Heidbreder can describe for you the financial losses TDS suffered and the mad scramble to repair the damage on several fronts, including Bandag's credibility with the dealer network. "We've turned the corner now," he says, but it was a mess.

A phrase in *The Case for Change* ultimately defined the relationship between Bandag and its dealers — the Bandag Strategic Alliance. It signaled that Bandag dealers could no longer service large fleets by themselves as a loose network but would have to coordinate their efforts, with leadership from Bandag, to affect purchasing decisions by the big

*"There is a counter-part to our dealer partners... our shareholder partners... But, if we need to lean one way or another, it will always be to the side of our dealers."*
— *Gene Seyb*

fleets. It meant a new relationship with corporate, now trying to provide a wide variety of fleet services. Here's how Bandag corporate communications positioned TDS vis-à-vis the Strategic Alliance: "A strong network of independent dealers, called the Strategic Alliance, allows Bandag to shift from the 'produce and distribute' paradigm prevalent throughout the industry, and focus on delivering differentiated value that meets customer needs. TDS strengthens the Strategic Alliance by ensuring uninterrupted distribution coverage, an important need of large regional and national fleet customers."

A follow-up document called *Checkpoint on Change* in 2002 observed: "One of the major reasons for dealers' animosity toward Bandag in the mid-'90s was our practice of adding additional franchised dealers into geography already covered by existing dealers. While this practice was essential to satisfy our investors, existing dealers resented having to compete with new Bandag dealers.

Jimmy Pickle looks o as Martin welcome Minnie Pearl to Universal Tire ope house even

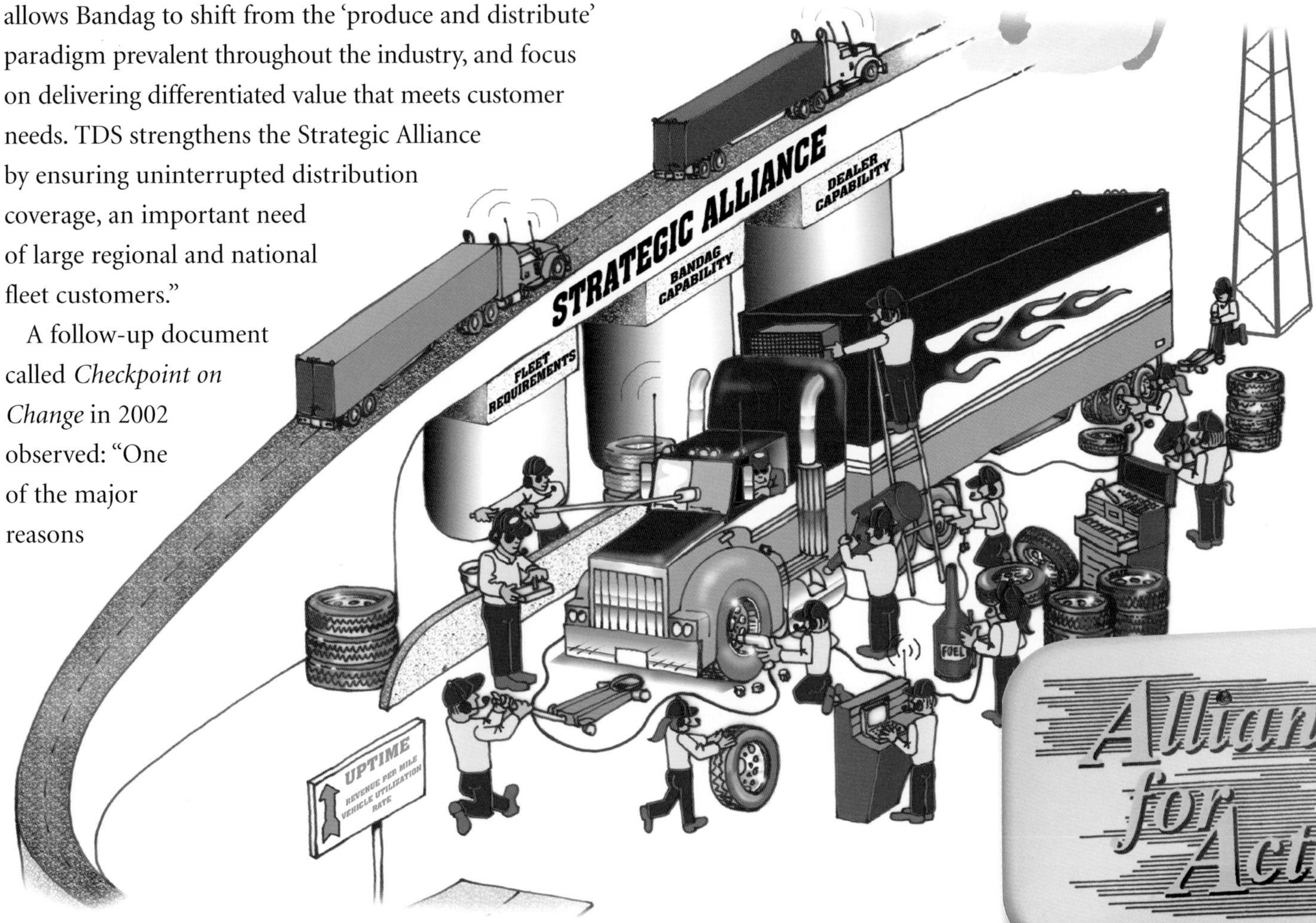

This illustration was part of an educational campaign explaining potential benefits of participation in the Bandag Strategic Alliance.

Wearing the Alliance for Action pin at the business conference was one way to show your support for the new way of working with dealers.

When Bandag announced the Strategic Alliance, Bandag committed to discontinue the practice of growing our business strictly through adding distribution and asked dealers in return to cover their marketplaces more aggressively."

The annual business conference in 1999 had brought matters to a head. In one of the most dramatic speeches Martin Carver ever made, he told the dealers: "If by now you don't think we've demonstrated our trust (through the purchase and formation of TDS), I don't now what more we can do. No one else in the industry has made such a commitment to you. That's because no one but Bandag cares so much for your independence and prosperity. The train is leaving the station and the ticket to ride is a commitment to follow a plan to change the behavior of your business. But please, don't waste our time if you're not willing to climb on board."

Well, many dealers did change their businesses, committing to Bandag's plan because it was the best for their independence. In other cases, dealerships refused to "get on the train" and left the Alliance, not to be replaced.

Reflecting the intense commitment to succeed that has always characterized Bandag, real progress was made in transforming the dealer network into a true strategic sales and distribution force. *Checkpoint on Change* proclaimed: "Building the foundation for the Bandag Strategic Alliance was a central focus of our efforts, and we've achieved

Evening entertainment at the Bandag business conferences featured top entertainers like John Denver, the Pointer Sisters and Alabama. Chubby Checker brought the crowd to its feet at this show.

At Bandag Business conferences Martin Carver delivered business messages, forecasts and motivational stories. His personal message in Phoenix in 2006 described his father and his passion for the business.

Bandag's list of featured guest speakers at Business Conferences included Art Linkletter in 1979.

remarkable success. Today, Bandag dealers and Bandag are truly interdependent and more trust exists in the Alliance than at any time in our history."

The foundation for that greater trust was the attention Bandag gave to refining every aspect of doing business. Offering high performing tread products and innovative retreading equipment was just the beginning. Bandag strengthened its "Package of Value" to dealers by redesigning and interconnecting every component of the Bandag Franchise Model to provide whole new benefits to the dealers. The most revolutionary of these components, the Bandag Financial Model, enabled Bandag dealers to diagnose which parts of their business offered the most profit-building potential, and that in turn helped dealers keep their independence.

As Bandag approached its 50th anniversary year, the Bandag Strategic Alliance was alive and well.

When Marty Carver talks about future challenges facing Bandag and the Strategic Alliance under Bridgestone ownership, he is anything but pessimistic. "This company has always been about meeting challenges through innovation. Now we just have to figure out how to provide a wider range of services in a fully coordinated fashion — everything the trucking industry needs. We'll figure out ways to do that better than the competition. We always have." ▪

LWAYS OUT FRONT.SM

## Roadway Outsources to Bandag

Getting truck fleets to outsource tire and other services was Bandag's most ambitious goal of the 1990s. Perhaps the best example of outsourcing in the tire industry — one that proved Bandag could handle tire services for anybody — was the agreement inked in 1999 by Roadway Express, Inc., and Tire Management Solutions, Inc. (TMS), a Bandag subsidiary.

It was a remarkable agreement because of the sheer size of Roadway, a fleet with 10,000 tractors and more than 35,000 trailers. Bandag assumed total responsibility to manage and maintain the tires at 400 terminals nationwide, 24 hours a day, seven days a week.

Dick Deardorff, Roadway's vice president of maintenance and corporate service, said, "We wanted to get out of the tire business and the whole host of responsibilities associated with being in the tire business."

His predecessor, Bill Demastus, had been associated with Bandag over many years through earlier tire management programs and was intimately known by many dealers.
In the early negotiations, Bill set the tone by making a simple statement: "I want my tire management outsourcing supplier to do two things in this contract — one, make sure that my vehicles have maximum uptime to deliver my contracted goods and, two, ensure that I have good performing tire products that meet DOT requirements. I don't want those headaches anymore."

Deardorff credited the Bandag Strategic Alliance for the seamless transition. "While TMS made sure the proper administration was in place, it was the network of independent

Bandag dealers that made sure the tires on our trucks were ready to deliver the maximum amount of uptime and safety."

Deardorff was convinced outsourcing would benefit other fleets. "It's out-of-the-box thinking and a totally different way of approaching the traditional methods of tire management. There needs to be openness and mutual trust between the transportation company and the tire management provider. Roadway and Bandag have had a long history and relationship to set the stage for this innovative approach to a fleet's tire management needs. If the economics make sense for the fleet and the provider, there is a good chance it will work for the fleet because it frees you up to focus on your core business."

Of course, Bandag agreed with Deardorff. The first two years were a bit bumpy, but after all, Bandag and Roadway were blazing a new trail. The next two years saw success for tire management outsourcing. Unfortunately, the deal ended when Roadway Express was bought out by Yellow Freight in 2004. While Roadway's desire to continue the TMS program was clearly stated, the different purchasing philosophy of the parent company Yellow Freight prevailed in the end. ▪

Outsourcing fleet tire programs to the Bandag Strategic Alliance was out-of-the-box thinking that paid huge dividends for the Bandag dealer base.

Bertis E. McGrif
founded McGri
Treading Compan
in the early '70
After experimentin
with anothe
retreading bran
McGriff solidifie
his commitmen
to Bandag a
the premiu
retread bran

McGriff started as a service station attendant in 1946. He soon became manager and before long he owned a successful tire company in Cullman, Alabama.

Martin Carver cuts the ribbon celebrating the reopening of the Bandag plant in Griffin, Georgia, which had burned down in 1983.

## Bandag Shows Its Compassion

So many of the Bandag employees you talk to emphasize, without prodding, the family atmosphere that has persisted over the years in the face of tremendous growth. They laud a culture where people count perhaps even more than the bottom line.

Gary Carlson, who held many different jobs at Bandag, knows up close the genuine people-oriented attitude that started with Roy Carver and continued to be encouraged by his son, Martin.

Carlson was plant manager at the Griffin, Ga., plant, which burned to the ground in 1983.

"It was colder than normal, and water lines froze. A fire started in the manufacturing plant, which was attached to the warehouse," Carlson says. "The roof caught fire, and because the water line was frozen, the sprinkler system didn't go off right away. Once a rubber fire starts, it's hard to put out."

Carlson said Bandag was deeply concerned about the people who had lost their jobs, their livelihood in ashes. "I knew those people, many of us at Bandag did, and we decided we couldn't just let them go down. So we lined up people in the community to help in various ways. We had good relations with other companies — Marty always insisted that we be active with the Chamber and other community activities — so we urged them to hire our people on. Of course, they couldn't always match what we had been paying, so Bandag paid the difference."

Carlson says they got the plant rebuilt in record time, about 18 months. "And 95 percent of the employees came back to work with us. I still get emotional when I think about Bandag's big heart and those workers' loyalty." ▪

## THE ANATOMY OF A NEW TREAD DESIGN

Tread design molds for Bandag designs are cast at Kendon, a Bandag-owned facility in Muncie, Indiana. These craftsmen take pride in the work, and excel in their performance.

The communities in and around Bandag facilities have benefited from Bandag, whether it was refurbishing a bus for the Salvation Army, promoting educational opportunities for children or just cleaning up the city.

Service has been a hallmark for Bandag. At the Business Conference dealers who have achieved major milestones are celebrated and applauded by their peers.

Michael M. Golightly & Associates, Inc. of Flagstaff, Arizona, celebrated 15 years as a Bandag dealer.

Pomp's Tire accepted service awards at many Bandag Conferences because of the many franchised locations they have established throughout the Midwest.

Canton Bandag Co., a veteran dealership, also accepted its 40-year award in 2002.

Elliott's Tire Service of Butler, Pennsylvania., a long-time dealer, accepted its 40-year award in Rancho Mirage in 2002.

The FCR™ product launch, which began Bandag's Application Specific product line, included a massive press conference in Muscatine — a rarity for any Bandag marketing campaign.

Premier Bandag was among the first dealerships to attain ISO 9001:2000 certification. From initial inspection through repairs and finished product, a quality management system provides fleets with a consistent service experience.

These dealers were some of many who shared their success stories in Bandag's *Profit & Opportunity* newsletter for the benefit of all Bandag dealers.

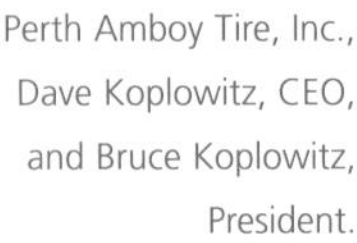

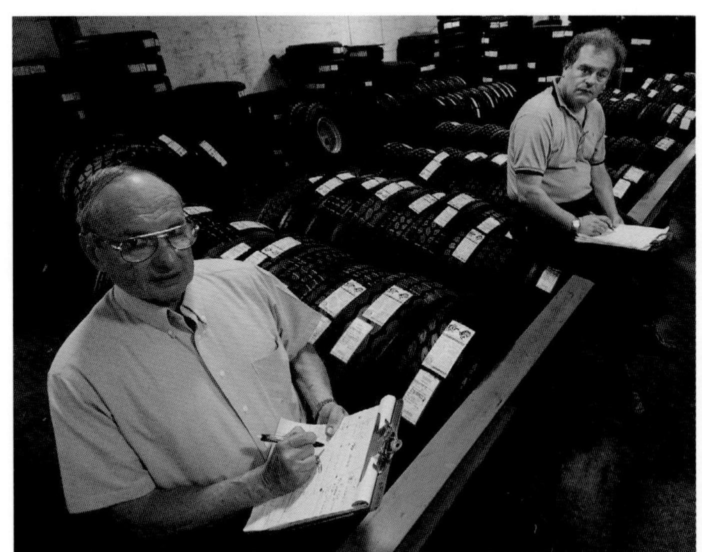

Perth Amboy Tire, Inc., Dave Koplowitz, CEO, and Bruce Koplowitz, President.

Rick Davis, commercial sales representative for Best One Fleet Service, uses the Bandag® Fleet Analyzer to collect and sort data for his fleet customers.

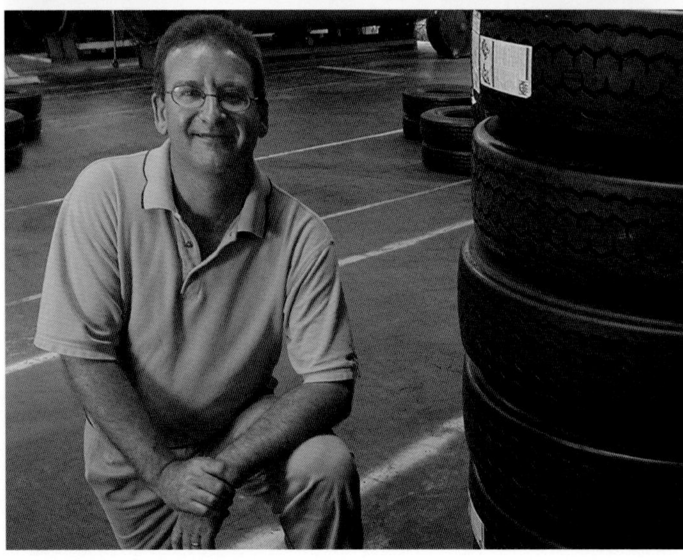

Scott Moore, General Manager of GCR Tire Centers.

Steve Burhenn, Executive VP and Chief Revenue Officer of Becker Tire, is always available to do a scrap tire analysis for a customer.

Doug Underwood of DOT Foods (center) depends on John House (left) and John Napier of Tommy House Tire to provide service, quality products, timely deliveries and help in cost control. Tommy House Tire was founded in 1955 by Thomas J. House.

Most Bandag franchises are independently-run businesses, like Sullivan Tire of North Attleboro, Massachusetts.

Jim McCurdy, vice president, Maine Commercial Tire of Bangor, Maine, provides hands-on tire management advice to a customer.

Freddy DeJesus and family of Custom Bandag is another example of an independent family-owned franchise.

Tri-Hi Transportation, a Merrill, Wisconsin fleet, listened closely to its Bandag dealer, Pomp's Tire, and moved to wide-based singles. Not only did the Bandag® retreads perform better than new tires, but they saved money too!

Martin Carver a
Mr. Rene Suarez
Llantas Vifrio S
Guatemala (wh
the son of the ow
of this dealersh
celebrate 45 ye
with Band

Bandag graphics were proudly displayed in businesses all around the world!

Jim Wochinske, president of Pomp's Tire, was always looking for new ways to leverage the Bandag brand.

BANDAG INCORPORATED WORLD HEADQUARTERS
45 years

A typical Speedco store features drive-through lube bays and dedicated tire lanes, ensuring fast, dependable service for truckers operating on major interstate highways.

## Speedco Broadens Bandag Services

In line with its commitment to adding trucking services, Bandag in 2004 acquired an 87.5 percent interest in Speedco, Inc., a nationwide quick-lube truck service company, from its founders and Shell Oil Products U.S.

Commenting on the purchase of Speedco, which also now provides on-highway tire repair and replacement, Martin Carver said: "Lubrication and tires are the trucking industry's two most frequent preventive maintenance needs. Given Bandag's and Speedco's respective leadership in their service sectors, the strategic fit is excellent. Speedco's service reputation and nationwide, on-highway presence create a solid platform for the expanded delivery of en-route maintenance services both now and in years to come."

Speedco is young — founded in the mid-'90s — and aggressive. Its slogan is, "No Slowing Down." Here's one of its marketing messages: "Out here [on the highway], every second counts. No one knows that better than Speedco. Our mission is simple: Get you back on the road faster than anyone else. That means quality lube and tire service in around 30 minutes. That means a can-do spirit you can count on at every location. No hassles. No excuses. No slowing down. Buckle up. You're in Speedco country now."

Warren Heidbreder, Bandag's former CFO, says: "Retreading is now a mature business; it's slow growth. So how do we turn ourselves back into a growth business? It's by finding related and growing businesses with a valid model, complementary to us so that we can cross-sell." He says the Speedco acquisition is a real plus because it offers the capability to serve customers we already have.

With 50 locations throughout the country by mid 2007, Speedco improves services to customers every year, opening new stores, installing better oil change equipment and selling an increasing volume of new tires as well as Bandag® retreads.

Interestingly, considering Bandag's historic interest in racing, Speedco is active in car, truck and drag racing. And it knows how to promote itself to people who love things on wheels. Speedco teamed up with Orange County Choppers to create the custom-built Speedco Chopper as part of the "Tribute to the American Trucker" at the 2006 Mid-America Trucking Show. The snazzy bike and surrounding hoopla raised $100,000 for charity.

It all sounds like Bandag in its young and hungry days. No wonder Carver said the two companies were an excellent fit. ▪

Custom built by the legendary Orange County Choppers, the Speedco Chopper was part of the "Tribute to the American Trucker" celebration at the 2006 Mid-America Trucking Show. Speedco then took the Chopper and its one-of-a-kind rig on a nationwide tour to help raise funds for the Make-A-Wish Foundation.

# 1957-2007

bandag®

50 bandag ESTABLISHED 1957

# REVOLUTIONS

## *Bandag's 50 Years of Innovation in the Tire Industry*

TIMELINE

**December 1957**: Roy Carver acquires North American rights to the Bandag retreading system from Bernard Anton Nowak in Darmstadt, Germany, and becomes president and general manager of Bandag, Incorporated.

## 1957

**January 1958**: Carver sets up a finishing line in a vacant sauerkraut factory on the edge of Muscatine, Iowa, using rubber from Nowak's small plant in Germany and later from a company in Akron, Ohio. Carver Pump Co. in Muscatine and other suppliers make the equipment.

Plant 2 in Muscatine becomes Bandag's first rubber plant.

Bandag's corporate employees are housed on upper floor of Carver Pump building at 1056 Hershey St., Muscatine. Other employees share space with Carver Foundry Products and Carver Pump Co.

Bandag dealer shop can be purchased for under $8,000 — everything from shop rags to bonding room — to retread 15 tires a day.

**June 1958**: Barely six months after acquiring North American rights, Carver establishes first franchised dealer.

**September 1958**: William Bennington named president of Bandag, Incorporated.

**June 1959**: Ambrosiani Brothers, San Juan, Puerto Rico, becomes first international franchised dealership.

Bandag also signs on first European dealer, A.B. Stockholm, Stockholm, Sweden.

## 1960

**January 1960**: Pressure chamber added to equipment line.

Bandag begins dealer services with Bandag employees trained to help dealers solve production problems.

**November 1960**: Roy Carver becomes president and chairman of the board of Bandag, Incorporated.

**January 1961**: World rights to Bandag retread system purchased from Bernard Nowak's heirs.

First tread press installed at Plant 2, pressing tread in 30-foot lengths, six pieces at a time; first designs are Highway, Cross Bar and HiSpeed.

Requiring more capital, Carver flies to dealerships and raises $50,000.

**October 1961**: Carver hires Harold Vischer to lead sales organization.

**January 1962**: It's make or break for Bandag, with employees working seven days a week.

Herb Roelle, a Bandag employee, is a major player in the design and building of the first Bandag buffer.

Tyrecappers, Durban, becomes first South African dealer.

**November 1962**: Bandag Cold Process in Sydney becomes first Australian dealer.

**January 1963**: Carver develops flexible rubber curing envelope, first key manufacturing idea introduced by Bandag; it solves many curing problems and eliminates heavy, expensive, metal curing bands.

Ed Brodie develops single-ply cushion gum, significantly improving reliability in retread production and solving the nagging bonding problems.

**January 1964**: Bandag Research & Development sets up in red brick house next to Plant 2 in Muscatine.

## 1965

**April 1966**: Carver accepts U.S. Presidential "E" award for Bandag's contributions to U.S. export expansion program.

**August 1966**: Stephen A. Keller named president of Bandag, Incorporated.

**December 1966**: Tread shipments domestic and international total 6,744,000 pounds.

Sales total $5,307,000.

**February 1967**: Bandag equipment plant moves to present location, 16,800-square-foot building in Muscatine.

**November 1967**: Bandag Canada LTD, company's first tread-rubber plant besides Muscatine, begins production in Shawinigan, Quebec.

**January 1968**: Bandag stock first offered to public at $12 per share.

Second tread rubber plant built in Oxford, N.C.

**December 1968**: Bandag has three-for-one stock split.

Bandag has franchised dealers in 25 countries.

**October 1969**: First Semi-Automatic Builder delivered by pickup truck to Chicago Bandag.

## 1970

**January 1970**: First tread rubber produced in Eureka, South Africa.

**March 1970**: Bandag mono-rail system introduced to speed up production in dealers' retread shops.

**October 1970**: Lanklaar, Belgium, tread rubber plant starts production.

**December 1970**: Bandag stock splits two for one.

**January 1971**: R&D Center and warehouse completed in Muscatine at Progress Park.

Oxford, N.C., plant expanded.

Abilene, Tex., tread rubber plant built.

**June 1971**: First stockholder meeting held at Hotel Muscatine. Board members present include Roy Carver, Eugene Seyb, Harold Vischer, William Cory, Steve Keller, Lucille Carver and Edgar Jannotta.

**November 1971**: Bandag stocks split three for two.

**January 1972**: Bandag listed on New York Stock Exchange.

Plant 5 completed in Muscatine.

Bandag franchised dealers now in 60 countries.

**February 1972**: Bandag adds "hot line" to help truckers locate nearest Bandag dealer with a toll-free number.

**November 1972**: New 53,500 square-foot Plant 5 tread rubber plant joined to warehouse and distribution center.

**January 1973**: Bob Seivert and Bill Loughran put Banda retreads to the test at Baja 500, first tim Bandag® retreads us for road racing; spar tire never touches the ground.

**April 1973**: Bandag R&D person retread carrier-based jet aircraft tires.

**July 1973**: At Pike's Peak Hill Cl Bob Seivert breaks u vehicle class records 13:41.3 minutes usi Bandag® retreads.

**November 1973**: Bandag purchases Master Processing Corp., Long Beach, Calif., custom rubbe compounder and producer of speciali rubber products for industrial use, advar Bandag R&D in rub compounding.

**anuary 1993**:
3andag New Zealand
.td., becomes first
3andag corporate-
owned manufacturer
of tread rubber to
win internationally
recognized ISO 9002
quality certification.

**May 1993**:
Bandag acquires Kendon
of Muncie, Ind., making
it exclusive tread mold
supplier to Bandag.

**ry 1992**:
r-one Bandag
plit.

**1992**:
g signs on in
first franchise
n year later.

**nber 1992**:
vards Deming
g begins, with
nployees learning
osophy and
ement system.

**January 1994**:
Bandag granted 17-year U.S. product patent for Eclipse System tread, culminating six-year project.

**April 1994**:
Set of Eclipse System retreads logs 496,917 miles.

**October 1995**:
Case for Change document provides overview of changes in North American trucking industry and new directions for Bandag.

**February 1996**:
Bandag Strategic Alliance announced at Business Conference.

**May 1996**:
Bandag Alliance Advisory Council formed.

**August 1996**:
Launch of Application Specific Product Strategy with introduction of FCR™ series treads.

**September 1996**:
Bandag do Brazil gets ISO-9002 accreditation.

**December 1996**:
Tread shipments total 378,858,000 pounds.

Sales $756,925,000.

**August 1997**:
Groundbreaking ceremony held for new Learning Center facility in Muscatine.

**September 1997**:
Tire Distribution Systems, Inc., newly formed, wholly-owned subsidiary of Bandag, Incorporated,. TDS, comprising five Bandag dealerships when merged, posted 1996 sales of $366 million.

**October 1997**:
Bandag has plants in following locations: Abilene, Tex.; Campinas, Brazil; Caracas, Venezuela; Chino, Calif.; Colombo, Sri Lanka; Griffin, Ga; Jakart, Indonesia; Johnannesburg, South Africa; Kuala Lumpur, Malaysia; Lanklaar, Belgium; Leon, Mexico; Muncie, Ind.; Muscatine, Iowa; New Delhi, India; Oxford, N. C.; Queensland, Australia; Shawinigan, Canada; and Vicksburg, Miss.

Griffin plant gets 1S0-9002 accreditation.

**December 1997**:
Bandag has 1,279 franchised dealer shops in 121 countries.

Sales $822,523,000.

Bandag celebrates 40 years of operations.

**February 1998**:
Bandag introduces Bandag Financial Model to dealers at Bandag Alliance Business Conference.

**March 1998**:
Bandag introduces TMS (Tire Management Solutions) with Mike Tirona as president.

**April 1998**:
Bandag and TCI Tire Centers, Inc., with 16 retread manufacturing locations, end franchise relationship.

**October 1998**:
Bandag closes Plant 2, first rubber manufacturing plant, "where it all began."

Envelope, arc rings, OTR tread and cushion operation from Plant 2 move to Bandag-Long Beach (BLC).

**November 1998**:
Bandag do Brazil begins production at new rubber manufacturing facility in Mafra.

**December 1998**:
Bandag holds first training class in the new Bandag Learning Center in Muscatine.

Sales $1,059,669,000.

**March 1999**:
Bandag opens doors to new Bandag Learning Center.

TMS signs contract with Roadway to own and manage all of its tire products and services.

**May 1999**:
Bandag South Africa launches their first tread product, called HBR, tread replacing Highway tread.

**August 1999**:
Bandag manufacturing facilities worldwide complete all assignments in quality assurance standards to become ISO 9002 Certified.

**September 1999**:
Bandag files lawsuit against Michelin Retread Technologies (MRTI) and Michelin North America (MNA) to protect strength of franchise and preserve Bandag distribution channel.

**December 1999**:
Plant 5, Bandag's manufacturing facility in Muscatine, closes.

Sales $1,012,665,000.

**January 2000**:
J.J. Seiter, president of TDS, retires and Sam Ferrise, Chief Operating Officer (COO) of Bandag, named TDS president.

**February 2000**:
Bandag launches three new pieces of equipment — Model 5400 OSM™ Tire Builder; 7400 INSIGHT® Casing Analyzer and Model 6400 Extruder at Bandag Alliance Business Conference.

**April 2000**:
Bandag receives exemption from Iowa's Franchise Law which will provide better protection for franchise agreements.

**July 2000**:
Bandag-Europe introduces Eurofleet, pan-European independent tire service network.

**September 2000**:
Bandag launches two new tread products (FuelTech® Drive and FuelTech® Trailer) using a new compound called Synergy.

**November 2000**:
Bandag's North American operations become union-free.

**December 2000**:
Sales $996,059,000.

**September 2001**:
Mike Tirona named vice president and general manager of Europe Operations.

TMS is realigned.

John McErlane named president of TDS.

**October 2001**:
Bandag phases out production at Chino manufacturing facility in California.

**February 2002**:
Bandag launches first-of-its-kind Fleet Symposium for CEOs and top executives of North American Fleets.

Bandag launches ISO 9001-2000 certification program for dealers; Westover Bandag of Chicopee, Mass., is first to become certified.

**July 2002**:
Bandag launches Checkpoint On Change communication program, which introduces new "vehicle-centric" vision for Bandag.

**February 2003**:
New computerized "hands free" 8400 Buffer is launched at Business Conference.

**August 2003**:
Bandag-Manugistics Team recognized by *Start* magazine for supply chain performance through technology.

Bandag opens third-party-operated warehouse in Tximshatui, Kowloon, Hong Kong.

**December 2003**:
Sales $826,354,000.

**February 2004**:
Bandag acquires 87.5 percent majority interest in Speedco, Inc., North America's leading quick-service truck lubrication business, from its founders and Shell Oil Products US.

**March 2004**:
Bandag's Equipment Plant achieves ISO Registration making all Bandag manufacturing locations ISO Certified.

Bandag-Europe changes name from: Eastern Hemisphere Retreading Division (EHRD) to EMEA Business Unit (Europe, Middle East, and Africa).

**May 2004**:
Bandag announces that Yellow Roadway Corporation will end outsourcing relationship with Roadway Express.

**June 2004**:
Speedco opens first tire lanes at new El Paso, Tex., location.

Speedco acquires assets of six Speedco Truck Lube locations from their licensee PM Express.

**October 2004**:
Bandag becomes Volvo's preferred Pan-European Truck Shop supplier; Volvo is world's second-largest producer of heavy trucks.

**November 2004**:
Bandag sells its South African Operation to local management, changing name of new business to Bandag Southern Africa (Pty) Ltd.

**December 2004**:
Bandag announces new outsource tire management services agreement with U.S. Xpress, however agreement would end in 2006.

Sales: $864,343,000.

**January 2005**:
Bandag creates new Vision for company: "We will be the leading provider of premium tire management and vehicle maintenance solutions to the transportation industry."

Bandag launches new product line called Continuum® brand precured retreading materials for off-the-road (OTR) market.

**July 2005**:
Bandag Bullet, world's fastest truck from Australia, sets world record for conventionally powered truck, achieving average speed of 182.14 kph over one kilometer from standing start.

**October 2005**:
Bandag acquires Maintenance IO, consulting firm specializing in fleet maintenance processes that improve efficiency and cost management.

**December 2005**:
Sales: $914,640,000.

1995

2000

2005

2007

**March 2006**:
Speedco sponsors tribute to American Trucker at the Mid America Truck Show in Kentucky and unveils Speedco Chopper built by Orange County Choppers.

**April 2006**:
Bandag acquires Trucklube 1, a leading provider of truck repair and maintenance services.

John McErlane named vice president of North America Operations and Mark Winkler named vice president of Vehicle Services reporting to Martin Carver, chairman and CEO.

**June 2006**:
Bandag closes Shawinigan Plant in Quebec; this plant was opened in 1967 and was company's first tread rubber plant outside Muscatine.

**December 2006**:
Bandag and tire maker Bridgestone Americas Holding, Inc., jointly announce that they have entered a merger agreement by which Bridgestone Americas will buy Bandag for $1.05 billion in cash.

**April 2007**:
Bandag shareholders approve the sale of Bandag, Incorporated to Bridgestone Americas Holding, Inc.

**May 2007**:
Speedco opens its 50th store, in Whiteland, Indiana.

**June 2007**:
Bandag becomes Bridgestone Bandag, LLC, but continues to operate as "Bandag." A big "Day One" celebration takes place in Muscatine, Iowa, attended by Bandag employees, plus executives from Bridgestone Americas including Mark Emkes, chairman and CEO of BSA. Despite a terrible tornado that strikes Muscatine during the festivities, the celebra[tion] proceeds, culminating with Martin Carver turning over the key to the Bandag Bandit to new chairman, CEO and president, Saul A. Solomon.

GOLDEN SERVICE BANDAG CLUB

**nuary 1974**:
rker Collins named
esident and CEO of
ndag, Incorporated.

**arch 1974**:
ndag hot air balloon
outs at American
treaders Association's
uisville show. Balloon
ed for races, industry
de shows and
vertising and sales
omotions.

t dealer business
nference held in
waii.

**gust 1974**:
ution Packer, "rocket-
wered" dragster uses
00 pounds of thrust
each 300 mph in
rter mile and runs
ne set of Bandag®
eads all season.
lbuquerque, N.M.,
ution Packer sets
v land speed record
22.58 mph in 5.11
onds on Bandag®
eads.

**ptember 1974**:
d rubber and
ion gum
ufacturing plant
ns production
hino, Calif.

**January 1975**:
Tread rubber plant built in Griffin, Ga.

Denny Long, one of top five drivers in Sports Car Club America's 1974 ratings, races on Bandag Micro-Sipe® retreads.

**May 1975**:
Groundbreaking ceremony for Bandag World Headquarters in Muscatine.

**January 1976**:
Tyrone Malone sets world land speed record for diesel trucks at blistering 144 mph in his "Super Boss" Kenworth equipped with Bandag® retreads.

**November 1976**:
Bandag Training Center completed in Muscatine.

**December 1976**:
Tread shipments, domestic and international, total 135,703,000 pounds.

Sales for 1976 total $182,140,000.

**February 1977**:
Bandag holds an international business Conference in Rio De Janeiro.

**October 1977**:
Dedication of Bandag World Headquarters in Muscatine.

**May 1978**:
World's first 72-inch Bandag curing chamber shipped and installed at D&D Tire in Victoria, British Columbia, Canada.

**October 1978**:
Pierre R. Debroux named president and CEO of Bandag, Incorporated.

**December 1978**:
Bandag has 859 dealerships and franchises in 51 countries.

**January 1979**:
Ground-breaking ceremony for tread rubber plant in Mexico.

Bandag and Tyrone Malone begin featuring "Bandag Diesel Racing Team" at open houses and trade shows; truckers delight in seeing Malone do "burnouts" in Bandag-equipped "Super Boss."

Bandag® retreads win Baja 1000; Ken Rice and Hal Sealund winners of modified 4-wheel-drive class in specially prepared Ford Bronco with Bandag® retreads; 220 vehicles begin race, 32 finish.

**April 1979**:
Bandag introduces NDI® (Non-Destructive Inspection) Tire Casing Analyzer, using ultrasonic sound waves to detect hidden flaws in tire casings.

**April 1980**:
Harold Vischer retires. During his career at Bandag the company grew from fewer than 100 dealers to more than 900 dealers worldwide.

**November 1980**:
Charles Edwards named president & CEO of Bandag, Incorporated.

**January 1981**:
Employees move into building in Zaventem, Belgium.

**June 1981**:
Roy J. Carver dies in a hospital in Marbella, Spain, after heart attack.

Martin G. Carver named chairman of the board of Bandag, Incorporated.

**January 1982**:
Training facility in Brazil established.

**March 1982**:
Model 275 and 276 pressure chambers feature new DPC (differential pressure cure), cure system designed to improve quality of retreads and reduce production costs.

**May 1982**:
Martin G. Carver named president.

Tyrone Malone begins European promotional tour, taking Bandag-equipped "Super Boss" Racing Kenworth to Bandag open houses throughout Europe.

**April 1983**:
Record one million pounds of tread rubber sold in one day.

**May 1983**:
Martin G. Carver named chairman of board, CEO and president.

**December 1983**:
Seven-year-old, 100,000-square-foot Griffin tread plant is destroyed by fire, $13 million in damage.

**February 1984**:
HTR 4000 Tread Series released — T 4100, R4200, D4300, D4310 provided high performance on radial truck tires.

**April 1984**:
Bandag Dealer National Warranty Program kick-off.

**October 1984**:
Grand re-opening at Griffin rubber plant; new construction of plant began March 1, 1984.

**December 1984**:
Bandag do Brasil, Ltda., tread rubber plant opened to serve world's second largest market.

**February 1985**:
ARC sealing system unveiled at 1985 Bandag Business Conference. System eliminates curing rims, flanges and tubes, reduces cure time and manufacturing cost, eliminates most miscure problems.

**October 1985**:
Roy Carver is inaugural inductee to Tire Industry Hall of Fame, sponsored by National Tire and Retreaders Association and Private Brand Tire Group.

**February 1986**:
BOND (Buyer Oriented Network of Dealers) program launched, giving Bandag capacity to meet needs of national fleets.

**December 1986**:
Tread shipments — domestic/international — 214,698,000 pounds.

Sales $370,396,000.

**January 1987**:
Bandag stock splits two for one.

**January 1988**:
With Martin Carver at wheel, Bandag Bandit sets new world land speed record on Bandag® retreads at Bonneville Salt Flats, 150.918 miles per hour.

**July 1988**:
ETA (Emergency Tire Assistance) takes first call at 6:08 p.m.

**December 1988**:
Bandag has 1,043 franchised dealer shops in 103 countries.

**February 1989**:
Bandag recognized as one of "Great Companies of the '90s." Financial World magazine reviews strategies and tactics of more than 3,000 companies before choosing the 30 firms it believed most likely to prosper in coming decade. Listing puts Bandag in company of Ford, Chrysler, IBM, AT&T, MCI, Johnson & Johnson, Apple and American Express.

**May 1989**:
*Forbes* magazine ranks Bandag 488 in "Forbes 500" list.

**February 1991**:
Eclipse System, new system of products, services and tire technology created: tire that looks and performs like new tire, has warranty as good as new tire warranty and sold with highest level of service and technical assistance.

**November 1991**:
Employee involvement effort increases job satisfaction, productivity and "grass roots" problem-solving.

**Janu**
Two-f
stock

**June**
Banda
China
to ope

**Dece**
W. Ed
trainin
715 e
his ph
mana

1975

1980

1985

1990

T H E   P R E S I D E N T S   O F   B A N D A G

ROY J. CARVER
Founder and Chairman, 1957
President and General Manager, 1/58 – 9/58
President, 1961 – 6/2/1966

STEPHEN A. KELLER
President, 6/2/1966 – 1972

HARKER COLLINS
President, 1973 – 1976

EUGENE E. SEYB
President, 1977

PIERRE R. DEBROUX
President, 1978 – 1979

CHARLES E. EDWARDS
President, 1980 – 1982

MARTIN G. CARVER
Chairman, 1981 – 1983
Chairman, President and CEO, 5/25/83 – 5/31/07

SAUL A. SOLOMON
Chairman, CEO and President, 6/1/07 – present

WILLIAM BENNINGTON
President and General Manager, 9/58 – 12/58
President, 1959 – 1960
(no photo available)

Martin Carver's career at Bandag ended May 31, 2007. Of all his accomplishments perhaps the most significant is having taught a company and an industry that how you conduct business is arguably more important than the business itself.

BRIDGESTONE
World's Most
Trusted Retread

CHAPTER SIX:

NO DETOURS — THOUGHTS FROM MARK EMKES, CHAIRMAN AND CEO, BRIDGESTONE AMERICAS HOLDING, INC.

# BANDAG — THE ROAD AHEAD

*There is only one constant in life, and that is change. If you don't continually evolve as a business, you will get left behind. There's a reason these phrases are used so frequently in business conversations — they ring true every time. That is why I'm pleased that Bridgestone Americas has joined with Bandag, Incorporated. As the newest member of the global Bridgestone family of companies, Bridgestone Bandag, LLC will continue the proud legacy so clearly chronicled on the pages of this book.*

*On one hand, this relationship between Bridgestone Americas and Bandag signals a new road ahead. But this new alignment should also be viewed as a continuation of the solid foundation that was originally paved by Bandag's founder, Roy J. Carver. Carver's perseverance and passion molded Bandag into a dynamic company, one that Bridgestone Americas is proud to welcome into the Bridgestone global group of companies.*

The combination of our two companies is a natural fit signaling the beginning of an enhanced level of service and technology for our customers, while providing the same great level of quality that our customers have come to expect. By combining our businesses, we'll better serve our customers by offering a comprehensive tire maintenance solution, backed by a complete line of new and retread truck tire offerings.

Transportation companies actively seek tire management programs that start with premium new tires and take them

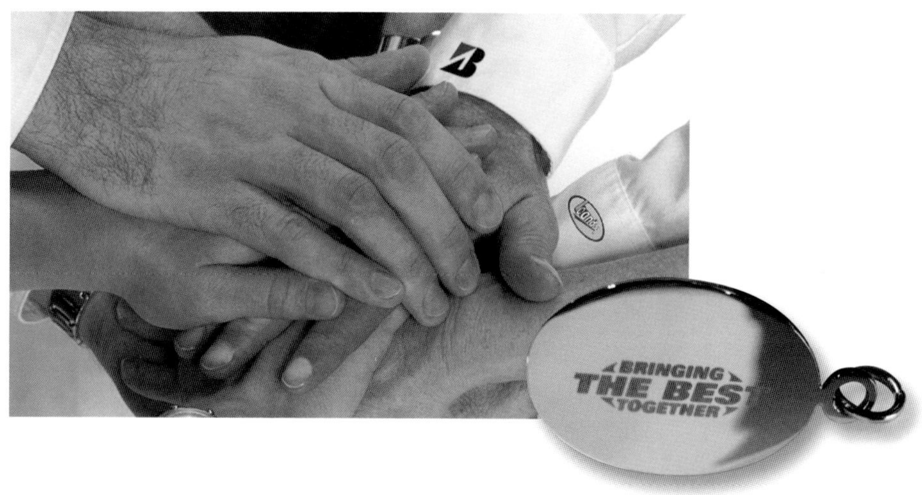

through the retread process. The joining of Bridgestone Americas, the largest subsidiary of the world's largest tire and rubber company, Bridgestone Corp., with Bandag, the premier global brand in retreading, provides our customers with a total tire offering, a streamlined way to manage their needs throughout a tire's life cycle.

The Bandag brand is respected throughout the world and is synonymous with leadership in quality, service and technology. We have great respect for Bandag's well-deserved reputation, for the people of Bandag and the company's relationships with fleet and dealer customers. This doesn't happen by accident. It is the passion, integrity and knowledge of the Bandag people that have made these relationships so successful.

Just days after the merger was complete, Bandag and Bridgestone truck and bus tire sales forces met to plan steps for bringing the best together into new sales offerings.

Bridgestone Firestone North America Tire provided this one-of-a-kind truck especially for the "Day One" festivities in Muscatine.

Warren Heidbreder, Mark Emkes, Saul Solomon and Martin Carver helped celebrate the merger on "Day One," figuratively the beginning of the next fifty years for Bandag.

As surely as truck wheels will keep turning, Bandag® retreads will be on them, delivering the trouble-free road miles the world now takes for granted.

Together, we will continue to be driven to success by one salient force — the commitment of our people to quality products, to improved technology, to innovation, and to the highest possible level of service to dealers and truckers around the world. If this sounds familiar, it may be because the first five chapters of this book are all about Bandag's 50-year tradition of honoring that very same commitment. And that is a tradition I am extremely honored to continue.

I look forward to enjoying the journey with all of you. ▪

stone®

# ACKNOWLEDGEMENTS

The book *Revolutions – Bandag's 50 Years of Innovation in the Tire Industry* would not have been possible without the tireless and unselfish contributions by many people. They include employees active and retired, dealers from around the world, and people whose lives may have been touched only briefly by Bandag's storied journey. It is with heartfelt gratitude that we thank each and every one for contributing their insight and memories to the words and pictures describing Bandag's first 50 years. However the ultimate gratitude must go to the legions of employees, dealers and customers, past and present, whose talent, time and determination shaped half a century of history which we know and admire as Bandag. Without you the preceding pages would have had nothing to say. Thank you.

— *Bandag Communications Group*